Michael Parker is the Headmaster of Newington College. He received Arts and Law degrees from the University of Sydney, has an MA in Philosophy and Education, and has published two novels and six books in the areas of Legal Studies, Philosophy in Schools, and English. He has also published three trade books with Ventura Press, including *Talk With Your Kids About Things That Matter*.

Fiona Morrison is an Associate Professor in English at UNSW, where she has taught and supervised in the areas of Australian and postcolonial literature, genre theory and modern rhetoric. Her recent books include *Christina Stead and the Matter of America* (2019) and *Time, Tide and History: Eleanor Dark's Fiction* (2024).

THINKING FOR YOURSELF

How to sharpen your ideas, decisions, arguments and views

MICHAEL PARKER
AND
FIONA MORRISON

First published in 2025 by Ventura Press
PO Box 780, Edgecliff NSW 2027 AUSTRALIA
www.venturapress.com.au

A catalogue record for this book is available from the National Library of Australia

Thinking for Yourself
ISBN: 978-1-7638320-3-9 (Print book)
ISBN: 978-1-7638320-4-6 (ebook)

Cover and internal design: Deborah Parry Graphics
Managing editor: Amanda Hemmings
Printed and bound in Australia by Griffin Press

Ventura Press acknowledges the Traditional Owners of the country on which we work, the Gadigal people of the Eora nation, and recognises their continuing connection to the land, waters and culture. We pay our respects to their Elders past, present and emerging.

The paper this book is printed on is certified against the Forest Stewardship Council® Standards. Griffin Press holds chain of custody certification SCS-COC-001185. FSC® promotes environmentally responsible, socially beneficial and economically viable management of the world's forests.

CONTENTS

Introduction 1

SECTION I: AWARENESS 15

Chapter 1: Getting started 17

What is critical thinking? 17

A short history of thinking 20

Types of reasoning 25

- Inductive reasoning 25
- Abductive reasoning 28
- Conditional (if/then) reasoning 32
- Deductive reasoning 36

The AC/DC method of Julian Baggini 37

Chapter 2: Everyday thinking about the world 39

Truth 42

- Theories of truth 42
- Why truth is contested 43
- Facts 45
- Opinions 50

Evidence 54

- Categories of evidence 54
- Standards and burden of proof 58
- Credibility and relying on experts 62
- Sources of information 65

Perils and precautions 67
Navigating generalisations 67
Fake news 71
The Dunning-Kruger effect 75
Occam's razor 78
Playing devil's advocate 81
Statistics – perils and pitfalls 84

Chapter 3: Building more skilful arguments 93
Claims 95
Premises and conclusions 95
Definitions 97
Issues 99
Evidence (again) 99
Counterarguments 100
Qualifiers 101
Inferences 101
Assumptions 102
Explanations 103
Is my argument any good: the Halpern method 104

SECTION II: CHALLENGES TO SOUND THINKING 107

Chapter 4: Cognitive biases 109
Fast and slow thinking 109
The resemblance bias and 'less is more' 113
The availability cascade 115
The anchoring effect 117
The planning fallacy 120
The priming effect 122
The law of small numbers 124

The sunk cost fallacy 126
The framing bias 128
The bike shed effect 130
Regret bias 132
The illusion of validity 134
The confirmation bias cluster 135
What you see is all there is 138
Peak end bias 140
A note on all the biases 143

Chapter 5: Thinking fallacies of relevance 145
Argument from false authority 147
The excluded middle 150
Arguments from emotion 153
Attacking the person 155
Straw men, weak men, hollow men and unfair extension 158
False analogy 161
The Galileo gambit 164
Red herrings 167
The genetic fallacy 170
Poisoning the well 173
Special pleading 176

Chapter 6: Thinking fallacies of presumption 179
The slippery slope 179
Unfalsifiability 183
Post hoc ergo propter hoc 186
Begging the question 189
Shifting the goalposts/No true Scotsman 192
Complex and loaded questions 195
Weasel words 197
Free speech and clichés that end an argument 200

SECTION III: REAL-TIME APPLICATION 203

Chapter 7: Making good decisions 205
Exploring possible solutions 207
Considering the alternatives 207
Using criteria 210
Evaluating your options 213
Necessary and sufficient conditions 213
Being consistent (most of the time) 216
Going from 'either/or' to 'both/and' thinking 219
Drawing distinctions 222
Using hypotheticals 226
Do it 228
Making 60-40 decisions 228
Prioritising (it's more than a list) 232
Learn from your decisions 236
Unknown unknowns and 'black swan' thinking 236
Avoiding the rush to judgement 241

Sidebar: The six thinking hats 244

Chapter 8: Being a fair-minded thinker 249
And so, we come to the end ... 255

Appendix: Deductive reasoning 257
Endnotes 261
Further reading 266
Acknowledgements 269
Index 271

INTRODUCTION

'The mind is like a parachute. It doesn't work if it is not open.'

Attributed to musician and composer Frank Zappa[1]

The need for books like this one really became clear to us about a decade ago when Michael accidentally taught a large group of 12-year-olds that the Earth might be flat. This goes down as the low point of a 30-plus year career of writing about, and teaching, philosophy, thinking and English. Michael has stopped having nightmares about it, but only in the last few months.

So, what happened? Ironically, he was trying to teach an earnest, well-behaved group about the importance of evidence, facts, opinions and sources. In a 'shoot fish in a barrel' sort of way, he brought up an American basketballer who was saying the Earth was flat. That led the group to a flat-Earth website that claimed 'good education tells you not to believe everything you read, but to do your own investigations instead. So now it's time to stop believing that the Earth is round and do your own investigations.' (We will not be providing the website details.) The website then provided a firehose of unmitigated drivel about the Earth being a disc with the North Pole at the centre and Antarctica spread all around the rim. Also, someone called General

Byrd went to Antarctica where he found something in 1954 *and never told anyone what it was*. The quality of the evidence went downhill from there. Its low point was that a lot of people had clicked on their website, so the Earth might be flat.

'So,' Michael said jauntily and confidently at the end of the session, 'who actually thinks the earth might be flat?'

A quarter of the group put their hands up.

After a few weeks of an epistemological crisis and a lot of lying down, a few things became clearer to us. Sound reasoning is not something you can take for granted. People at all sorts of thinking levels can stumble when it counts. It is not enough to assume that you can learn how to think critically just by hoping it bubbles up as you are learning something else. Critical thinking is better if it is spelt out in books like this. Books like this might not be enough … but they are a big step forward

Books like this are needed more now because there is so much more trash out there that needs to be filtered. That group of 12-year-olds would never have found the flat-Earth theory 20 years earlier. But now it's right there, just a click away. In addition, social media feeds, augmented by AI, can now feed us an increasingly rich diet of disinformation. We owe it to ourselves to give ourselves a fighting chance to think independently and well by having a sound idea about how good thinking works.

So, the two of us got to work extracting almost a hundred critical thinking techniques, tips and methods. We consulted a range of other works about thinking. We ranged through our 30 years of experience in embedding critical thinking in classes, lectures and tutorials. That's what you will find in this book. We want you to be more conscious of effective thinking and to understand its many benefits.

The techniques and methods in this book will help you:

- understand what sound and clear thinking looks like
- be conscious of your directed thinking when it appears (Section I)
- notice the roadblocks to skilful thinking (Section II)
- practise effective thinking habits so that sound thinking becomes more automatic and you avoid pitfalls of fuzzy thinking (Section III).

None of this is to say you don't already think. You do. From the moment you wake up, you make choices, deal with other people, hear the news and form opinions about the world around you. Indeed, you have been thinking soundly since well before kindergarten, so you have had a lot of practice; and most of what you learnt at school had reasoning at its base. The fact that you picked up this book probably means you are ahead of most people. Furthermore, a lot of brilliant people didn't have a 'how to think for yourself' book on their bedside table (Einstein, Marie Curie and Aristotle spring to mind). Sound thinking is an essential skill set, and one we can improve with focus and a bit of investigation and practice.

We hope this book will help you to optimise your thinking. It will speed it up (where necessary), slow it down (where necessary), clarify it and make it more effective. The book will give you terms and tools to make explicit some thinking that you might already have been using implicitly. It will give you other thinking techniques you had no idea about. If you take it seriously, reading this book will do more to sharpen your mind than almost anything else you could do in the same amount of time. And if you are reading this book a decade after attending Michael's accidental flat-Earth session, we hope it gives you the courage to splash out and buy a round-the-world plane ticket.

You can use this book in different ways. You could read it from start to finish. It is, however, designed as a handbook, so you should be able to open it anywhere and find something useful or interesting. Some of the most applied sections, such as 'making better decisions', are close to the end, and you may prefer to go straight to them.

TOP WAYS THIS BOOK CAN HELP YOU

TOP 5 for **putting together an excellent work presentation**

- Criteria (page 210)
- Distinctions (page 222)
- Consistency (page 216)
- Counterarguments (page 100)
- Straw men (page 158)

TOP 5 for **choosing to rent or buy a house**

- Necessary and sufficient conditions (page 213)
- Prioritising (page 232)
- Making 60-40 decisions (page 228)
- The slippery slope (page 179)
- The anchoring effect (page 117)

TOP 5 for **thinking about current affairs issues**

- Opinions (page 50)
- Credibility and relying on experts (page 62)
- Playing devil's advocate (page 81)
- The excluded middle (page 150)
- The confirmation bias cluster (page 135)

TOP 5 for **choosing which job to take**

- Using criteria (page 210)
- Considering the alternatives (page 207)
- Using hypotheticals (page 226)
- Arguments from emotion (page 153)
- The availability cascade (page 115)

TOP 5 for **choosing who to vote for**

- Argument from false authority (page 147)
- Poisoning the well (page 173)
- Facts (page 45)
- Evidence (page 54)
- Fake news (page 71)

TOP 5 for **working out if you are being taken for a ride**

- Arguments from emotion (page 153)
- Galileo gambit (page 164)
- Unfalsifiability (page 183)
- Occam's razor (page 78)
- The law of small numbers (page 124)

TOP 5 for **writing a good essay**

- Truth (page 42)
- Premises and conclusions (page 95)
- Issues (page 99)
- Evidence (page 54)
- Is my argument any good: the Halpern method (page 104)

TOP 4 for **working out where to go on holiday**

- Going from 'either/or' to 'both/and' thinking (page 219)
- Unknown unknowns and 'black swan' thinking (page 236)
- Making 60-40 decisions (page 228)
- Peak end bias (page 140)

TOP 5 for **becoming a better person**

- Going from 'either/or' to 'both/and' thinking (page 219)
- Opinions (page 50)
- Credibility and relying on experts (page 62)
- Assumptions (page 102)
- Being a fair-minded thinker (page 249)

TOP 5 for **demonstrating to 12-year-olds that the world is not flat**

- Occam's razor (page 78)
- Fake news (page 71)
- Opinions (page 50)
- Unfalsifiability (page 183)
- Galileo gambit (page 164)

CLEARER THINKING HELPS YOU AT WORK

The job types that are expanding require increasing levels of good thinking each day.

This list shows the skills that are in demand according to the World Economic Forum Future of Jobs Report 2023.[2] The very first is 'analytical thinking'.

Reading, writing and mathematics are way down at number 16! Individual employers attest that strong thinking skills are fundamental as well. When Laszlo Bock was the Senior Vice President in charge of hiring at Google, he said: 'The number one thing we look for is general cognitive ability, and it's not IQ. It's learning ability. It's the ability to process on the fly. It's the ability to pull together disparate bits of information.'[3]

It's clear: strong thinking skills will help you get a job, keep it and progress.

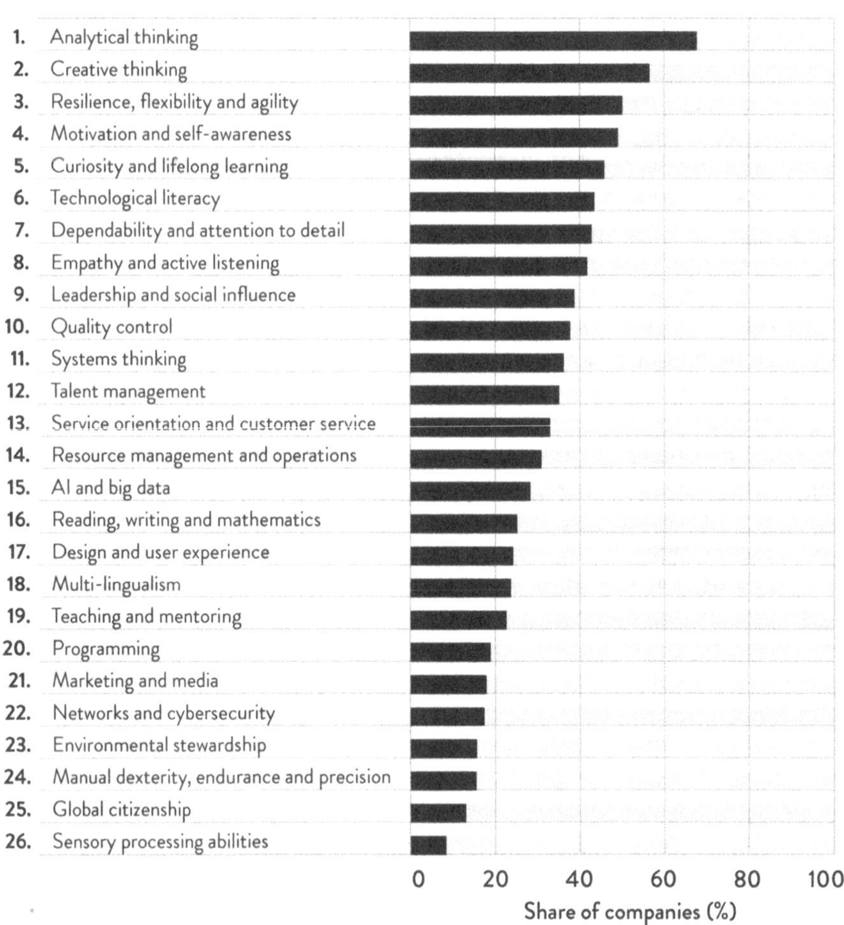

CLEARER THINKING HELPS YOU BE A GOOD CITIZEN IN A DEMOCRACY

Democracy is fragile. It has existed legitimately for only a few hundred years in a human history of millennia (with a brief experiment in Greece 2500 years ago). A strong democracy relies on people being informed and able to think for themselves. We owe it to ourselves, and to future generations, to be rigorous about how we think so we can process the complex and multifaceted issues that come our way to sustain and preserve this democracy. As Pericles said of people in ancient Athens: 'We do not say that a man who takes no interest in public affairs is a man who minds his own business. We say he has no business being here at all.'

While this seems a little stark, it does underscore our responsibilities as citizens.

It is becoming more and more difficult to get a clear window to the world from the internet and news sites. Troll farms and bots mean bad actors can flood outlets with so much wrong information and disinformation that people give up on discovering what is true and what isn't. Deep fakes, AI and video technology make it harder to rely on anything we see, let alone read. As chess grandmaster and Chairman of the Human Rights Foundation Garry Kasparov said: 'The point of modern propaganda isn't only to misinform or push an agenda. It is to exhaust your critical thinking, to annihilate truth.'[4]

Being able to think for ourselves and filter the reliable from the rubbish is more important and more difficult than ever.

It is better for everyone to be thoughtful rather than thoughtless. Not everyone needs a PhD in logic, but it would be terrific if almost everyone in a liberal democracy thought about their beliefs, possessed well-developed critical thinking skills and fostered curiosity.

CLEARER THINKING HELPS GIVE YOU A STRONGER CHARACTER

Clear thinking doesn't just help with individual decisions or opinions. It also helps us become the people we most want to be. It is about our character. Furthermore, the more power you have, the more your thinking is important for the sake of those who are affected by your decisions, as well as yourself. This could be the team you lead at work, your family or the company you run. For a very small handful of you, it might be the decision whether to invade another country or start a nuclear war, which makes your clear thinking very important for many, many other people (spoiler – the answer is almost always 'don't do it').

Richard Paul and Linda Elder write extensively about intellectual character, and we focus on this in chapter 8. They say that clear and critical thinking gives you more courage, humility, empathy, autonomy, resilience and integrity. This is a powerful combination.

Thinking clearly can also make you feel more in control. It allows you to do your best when making decisions and then be comfortable that you did the best job you could with the tools you had. Thinking critically about decisions doesn't guarantee right or happy choices, but it increases the *chance* of them. This, in itself, makes a proper study of critical thinking worth it.

CLEAR THINKING HELPS YOU EMPHASISE HUMAN THINKING IN THE ERA OF AI

We live in an era in which good, clear, independent, human thinking could be endangered, at risk from the far-reaching consequences of artificial intelligence (AI). Strengthening your independent thinking will allow you, at least, to buck this trend.

Let us explain further. We have spent thousands of years painstakingly working on thinking. We have learnt how to think better and better, particularly in the last century. We've created problems, but we've solved them too. On the cusp of the twenty-first century, we had more people being educated and more access to knowledge than ever before. It was hardly perfect, but it was heading in the right direction.

Much of that is now challenged by our own human willingness to outsource our thinking to AI. This is very different from previous advances in technology. In the past when we learnt to write instead of needing to keep information stored in our head, our capacity to remember might have been reduced, but our capacity to think was not. The move from physical books to Google might have challenged our capacity to research, but it didn't affect very much our capacity to think.

But generative AI does something very different. Fed a complex question, even in its current nascent development, it does almost all the thinking for you. People might think: 'I have this essay/work project to write. I'll just use AI to get me started with a few ideas'. Then they might think: 'Well, I have all these ideas. I'll just use AI to organise them in the best way possible'. Then they might think: 'Well, I have my essay/project, I'll just get AI to express it in a clear way'. Then they might think: 'I've written it, I'll just get AI to edit it'.

Individually, each of these tasks might be defensible as part of a workflow, but collectively, AI has done the whole job. The human intermediary has just filled in a few gaps along the way. And generative AI hasn't 'thought' a single thing in the process. We are outsourcing one of our core human functions to AI … and it doesn't even consciously think about it itself.

The consequences of generative AI are far greater than this. It can already solve complex scientific problems such as effective protein folding – but it can't tell us *how* it is doing it. Whatever process AI uses is beyond our rational capacity. In addition, unlike every other human invention, AI learns – and it learns exponentially. What people could have done in 100 years, AI can do in 10 years, then one year, then 26 weeks, then a fortnight, then 20 minutes. This is an incredible, but also troubling, development.

Furthermore, the possibility that AI could become conscious presents another series of existential challenges to humanity and our thinking. We will have created a conscious intelligence that is, in many ways, a trillion times smarter than us. If that happens, who will control whom? AI doesn't need consciousness to exercise control – merely a set of self-generated instructions and access to our online networks, including our finances, utilities and weapons.

In light of this we should at least clarify our own unique human qualities – our feelings, our emotions, our creativity and our critical thinking – and allow them to flourish. At this juncture, we can think better than ChatGPT, by the norms of good thinking. And we should.

Hopefully amongst using thinking to be more effective in your work, be a better citizen, make decisions, sharpen your opinions, improve your character and tackle AI, you have good reasons to keep reading. However, to make all this work, you might also have to do something after you put the book down. You might need to change.

THE HARD PART: CHANGING

Critical thinking can be hard. It's not the ideas themselves: if the ideas in this book were outdoor walks most of them would be graded 'easy/moderate'. But what do you do next if you apply critical thinking tools to ideas, beliefs or practices you hold dear and you find you have been misguided? Worse, what if you think you have been wrong for decades? Do you change your belief? Or do you decide to distrust the critical thinking tools that led you to this juncture?

Almost all of us are deeply affected and shaped by beliefs we have had since we were very young. These beliefs often didn't come to us through a process of rational thinking; they were handed to us by our parents, by what we watched and by what our friends said.

Some of those beliefs might not stack up. Time has moved on, your life experiences have increased, your context may have changed. Clear thinking might tell you that you need to change a belief, opinion or outlook. However, many people will not alter their practices or beliefs. Instead, they might choose to deride, pervert or redefine rational thinking. They might disdain the idea of listening to another point of view. They might even set themselves against education itself: consider phrases such as 'intellectuals in their ivory towers' or 'elites telling us how to live'. For some, critical thinking can seem suspect and threatening.

It shouldn't be.

If you do take on board all that the field of critical thinking has to teach, it does not lead to a life of confident fulfilment. Indeed, sometimes, applying critical thinking deeply can be frustrating. The destructiveness of some public discourse and the willingness of some people with power to abuse good arguments can become hard to bear. But knowing *explicitly* how to think well is still much, much better than the alternative. If someone offered you a blue pill that would immediately wipe out your capacity to think clearly and make you happy with every view proffered by your parents, employer, professor, pastor, political leader or teacher, would you take it? Probably not. Many – perhaps even most – people would prefer the frustration of independent thinking and the willingness to change to the blissful satisfaction of total credulity.

So read on …

Michael Parker and Fiona Morrison

SECTION I
AWARENESS

'Many people would sooner die than think.
In fact, they do.'

Philosopher Bertrand Russell[5]

CHAPTER 1

GETTING STARTED

WHAT IS CRITICAL THINKING?

Critical thinking is using your deliberative and careful reasoning to come to justifiable conclusions about your decisions and your beliefs.

There we go. We think this is short. And sharp. And hopefully quite good.

If that's all the definition you need, skip to the next section. However, if you would like to see us pit our pithy but workaday description against the Goliaths of twentieth century thinking, read on.

A clear notion of what has come to be known as critical thinking appeared in the early nineteenth century, around 1815 or so. The *Oxford English Dictionary* offers this definition: 'The objective, systematic and rational analysis and evaluation of factual evidence in order to form a judgement on a subject, issue, etc.'

As the field of critical thinking began to take shape, the influential figure of philosopher, psychologist and educator John Dewey (1859–1952) was key. He wrote about 'reflective thinking' in 1909 in the context of the clear importance of critical thinking for the purposes of education.

What follows is a series of definitions of critical thinking, starting with Dewey.

Who	**Definition**
John Dewey (1909)	'Active, persistent and careful consideration of a belief or supposed form of knowledge in the light of the grounds which support it and the further conclusions to which it tends.'[6]
Edward Glaser (1941)	'An attitude of being disposed to consider in a thoughtful way the problems and subjects that come in the range of one's experience. Knowledge of the methods of logical inquiry and reasoning and some skill in applying those methods.'[7]
Robert Ennis (1989)	'Critical thinking is reasonable reflective thinking that is focused on deciding what to believe or do.'[8]

Who	Definition
Peter Facione (1990)	'… purposeful, self-regulatory judgment which results in interpretation, analysis, evaluation, and inference, as well as explanation of the evidential, conceptual, methodological, criteriological, or contextual considerations upon which that judgment is based.'[9]
Richard Paul, Gerald Nosich and Linda Elder (1993)	'Critical thinking is that mode of thinking about any subject, context or problem, in which the thinker improves the quality of his or her thinking by skilfully taking charge of the structures inherent in thinking and imposing intellectual standards upon them (reasons, evaluation, clarification, credibility, argument, explanations, decisions).'[10]
Diane Halpern (2002)	'Critical thinking is the use of those cognitive skills or strategies that increase the probability of a desirable outcome. It is used to describe thinking that is purposeful, reasoned and goal-directed.'[11]

A SHORT HISTORY OF THINKING

Thinking critically has a long history; people have been thinking in organised ways for tens of thousands (if not hundreds of thousands) of years. People thought about how to kill that woolly mammoth. People deliberated about how to grow their crops instead of forage. People thought about how to get 100 people living in the same small community. People speculated about the lights in the sky. All of this was clear and directed thinking; it was not always just automatic or intuitive.

For all this time people were using *reason*, which is richly connected to the sound thinking faculties we use today. Reasoning required people to set aside feeling, intuition and habit and focus instead on a kind of self-aware and structured approach to what they thought they knew or what they would like to decide. They didn't have the same language, schools and critical thinking books that we do. We don't know exactly how they reasoned, but we can see it in its results: the domestication of animals, the creation of villages and towns, the rise of religion. As far as we know, of the hundreds of thousands of species on the planet, we are the only one who has evolved to reason in a formal way.

In the Western tradition, formal reasoning really developed in the fifth to fourth centuries BCE in Greece, thanks to giant figures such as Socrates, Aristotle and Plato. Greeks thought of reason in terms of the Greek word 'logos', which has many meanings including logic, explanation, speech, questioning, argument and explanation. Both Plato and Aristotle wrote about the practice of argument. Aristotle laid many of the foundation stones for both the art of rhetoric (the way we use and study visual, spoken and written language) in his work *Rhetoric*,[12] and the systems of formal logic in the *Organon*.[13] Plato, however, was quite suspicious of the practice of rhetoric in his dialogues

Gorgias and *Phaedrus*, because he saw it leading to a decline in values.[14] Socrates, who had been Plato's teacher, was worried about rhetoric as an art devoted to persuasion because he thought it interrupted the proper contemplation of truth. Later Roman philosophers and politicians regularly used, taught and followed their Greek predecessors, though for them the Greek 'logos' had a Latin version, 'ratio'. Lawyers and politicians used, tested and refined Aristotle's examples. They still do.

Confucian concepts of critical thinking in China involved 'li', which required each person to take knowledge and norms ('dao') to exercise judgement in individual situations. Thinking also needed to be underpinned by 'ren' – that is, ethical humanity.[15] Ancient Indian philosophy included 'Anviksiki', an investigative method based on critical thinking to explore different disciplines and issues.

So, throughout the world, reasoning was being used as part and parcel of a commitment to rationality. Rationality, which we associate with the West after the Renaissance, was an overall mindset, or even a values set. If you were committed to rationality, you were interested in ancient forms of logic and structure, you tended to be interested in different viewpoints, and you were keen to evaluate.

In the Middle Ages in Europe, the 'trivium' was often the focus of teaching, particularly in monasteries. The trivium was a combination of grammar, logic and rhetoric. The word 'trivium' means 'a crossroads where three roads meet', and the trivium was meant to support the four higher liberal arts of arithmetic, geometry, music and astronomy (quadrivium). These seven elements were the secular part of an education, delivered alongside religious instruction from the Bible.

The study of logic, rhetoric and thinking continued in the profusion of philosophy in the Western world in the few hundred years after the Renaissance. Formal logic became a large, dedicated and labyrinthine field of study akin to some branches of mathematics. Its strands included Rogerian rhetoric – a twentieth century form of reasoning based on finding common ground.

But 'how' to think was often buried in various different subjects. People could learn how to think scientifically, or how to think mathematically, or how to think philosophically by studying these subjects. In these cases, actually learning to think was merely a welcome by-product of learning to practise each discipline.

Sustained work was done in the late twentieth century to filter 'thinking' out of individual disciplines and make 'critical thinking' a standalone subject. In the 1970s, California mandated that its state universities teach critical thinking. This resulted in essential foundational work from academics such as Brooke Moore and Richard Parker, who wrote *Critical Thinking*, and Diane Halpern, who wrote *Thought and Knowledge*. The Centre for Critical Thinking, spearheaded by Richard Paul and Linda Elder, has had academics and thinkers spending decades working on the combination of critical thinking and intellectual character.

In the late 1970s, the Philosophy in Schools movement took critical thinking into the primary and secondary classrooms. Its founders, Matthew Lipman and Ann Margaret Sharp, wrote thousands of pages of activities for six- to 18-year-olds and came up with their own way of teaching them based on a 'community of inquiry'. In teaching philosophy with a focus on clear thinking they developed a pedagogy that was profound and long-lasting. Much of this work was picked up in Australia, where Philip Cam is a leading light. He has spent his career working on thinking in classrooms and produced a number of excellent books, among them *20 Thinking Tools*.

At the same time, a great deal of work was done on the physiological basis of much of our thinking and how, with the best will in the world, we can still fall prey to faulty thinking. The authority here was Daniel Kahneman (1934–2024), who won a Nobel Prize for his work, as well as his colleague Amos Tversky (1937–1996). Kahneman's bestselling book *Thinking, Fast and Slow* (2011) distils their insights, and one day he may well sit alongside Sigmund Freud, Charles Darwin and other giants who revealed startling new things to humanity. Chapter 4 of this book focuses on insights from the field to which Kahneman gave so much.

Recent years have seen a proliferation of material focused on thinking well in order to perform better. Some material was designed for university undergraduate courses. Other material was destined for professional bookstores. They all speak to a recognition that many people might not have been taught or exposed to the fundamental skill of thinking well at school or at university, but sense how important it could be in their daily lives. Some focus on self-help, others focus on tough love, some are optimistic, some are cynical; but all of them take a fundamental activity we do all the time – thinking – and turn the microscope onto what it is and how to do it better.

Where did the term critical thinking come from?

People these days often find the word 'critical' a bit misleading. It often summons up the idea of harsh negative judgements rather than the work of thoughtful and reasoned evaluation. Critics are assumed to be mean slanderers and fault-finders rather than judicious thinkers who engage analytically with what is being read, seen or heard.

The modern word 'critic' emerges from Greek, Latin and French meanings. They all relate to the capacity to discern and decide. Unsurprisingly, all three are related to making judgements. The *Oxford English Dictionary*, which traces the use of the word 'critic' through time, states that it is a person who works with critical analysis or evaluation (1586). This person typically engages in the study or analysis of texts (initially the Bible but later literary texts).

The word 'critical' came to play a clear role in science – and 'sticking the boot in' is not the meaning at all. In medicine, for example, 'critical' in 1556 indicated a crisis or decisive point, and in science, a point of transition from one condition to another (1808) – even a tipping point. You can see the continuation of the idea of discernment and decision from the classical meanings.

Then there is the word 'critique'. This is the French version of the Latin 'criticus' and the English 'critik/critic'. 'To critique' was to analyse, evaluate and comment on (to review) a literary text in 1752. 'Critique' only acquires a sense of negative judgement in English by the mid-twentieth century. 'Criticism' – as in 'literary criticism' – follows in these pathways. We need to rescue the word 'critical' from its fault-finding vibes. A judgement or evaluation might be negative, but it is the thoughtful engagement, close interpretation and high value for reasoned judgement that distinguishes criticism, rather than the negativity or grumpiness.

TYPES OF REASONING

To 'reason' describes a structured thinking process with distinct elements and terms and involving the application of logic. This means that the thinker works to determine whether something is truthful by pondering all the claims involved and the relationship between them. This can feel quite mathematical at times. Reasoning generally aims to arrive at a set of conclusions or a judgement.

There are different types of reasoning in critical thinking. Most of what we do is called 'inductive reasoning' and that is what most of this book is about. However, there are other, more formal, types too, called 'abductive' and 'deductive'. It's good to know about these structures and forms, even though you might not explicitly use them each day. They can put a spine into the body of your thinking – and even if other people can't see it, they should sense it is there.

Inductive reasoning

Inductive reasoning involves drawing a general principle from specific examples. Most of the reasoning we use each day is inductive, even though it isn't flawless. For example:

I go to work Monday.

I go to work Tuesday.

I go to work Wednesday.

Based on this evidence, I could draw the inductive conclusion that I go to work every day.

So, let's keep trying.

I go to work Thursday (check).

I go to work Friday (check).

I go to work Saturday (nope).

This shows that inductive reasoning is far from perfect.

Inductive reasoning often does work very well, despite the example above. We use it all the time to predict what happens in the world. The sun rose yesterday, it rose today, it's probably going to rise tomorrow. This isn't guaranteed, because it's possible the sun might blow up today or get sucked into a black hole midway through the evening. But based on previous evidence, you can be pretty confident in your general, inductive conclusion that the sun will rise again tomorrow. The premises of inductive reasoning support the conclusion, but don't prove it.[16]

In fact, a great deal of what we presume to be true is because of inductive reasoning. Its truth is a matter of degree (compared with more ironclad, deductive proofs such as 2+2=4, which we will talk about soon). Is the colleague who is mean to you most days going to be mean to you today? Unless they went into therapy last night, probably yes. Is the coffee shop that made you a great cup of coffee for the past 10 days going to make you a great cup of coffee today? Probably yes. Is the stock market that went up for the past 200 consecutive days going to go up today? Probably yes (but one day you are bound to be wrong). Without inductive reasoning we wouldn't be able to predict anything, and life would feel like an anxiety-inducing hellscape of randomness.

Inductive reasoning is also a key element in making some of the most important decisions in your life, including what job to take, whether to buy a house or rent, or whether to go to Botswana or the Amazon for your next holiday. Inductive reasoning won't be *all* you use (more on that later too), but it should be right up there.

The word used for a strong inductive argument is 'cogent'. Your belief that the train will be on time because it was on time for the past 10 days is cogent because it is very predictable. Your belief that the traffic light will turn to 'walk' as you approach it because it has turned to walk on the past 10 days is weaker and less cogent. It is just as likely you have been lucky, and it will be 'Don't walk' today.

Most statistics are another form of inductive reasoning. A poll that says only 30 per cent of people are going to vote for the prime minister's party based on 1000 responses allows you to predict a bad election for the prime minister's party once the millions of votes are counted. But you still can't be sure, because you are using specific responses to come to a general conclusion. Saying 'five out of 10 members of my family' believe the earth is flat does not mean half of the population of the country believes the earth is flat.

Inductive reasoning is a key way we think about the world.

TRY IT OUT

Which of these statements look like inductive reasoning, and which look like something else?

- I really liked the last 50 Monet paintings I saw – I will very probably like the next one I see.
- Parallel lines will never meet.
- None of us can find our wallets – I think we have been burgled.
- The Wallabies are on a winning streak, winning 10 out of their past 10 games, and I think they will win the next game.
- When I drink too much I get a hangover.
- All people are mortal, and Jane is a person, so Jane is mortal.

Abductive reasoning

Abductive reasoning is closely linked to inductive reasoning.

It is 7.00 am and you walk into the kitchen you cleaned the previous night. You know your brother had a shift starting at 6.30 am and left the house early. The place is a mess. Breakfast dishes are everywhere, cereal is spilt on the floor, the fridge door is open and beeping and there is cat food in the bowl.

'What happened?' you ask yourself. Did you sleepwalk? Has a robber broken in, stolen various breakfast condiments, left a mess, then kindly fed the cat in an act of remorse? Are all the plates and bowls actually people who have been cursed to live as crockery, *Beauty and the Beast*-style, who had a dance party last night before reverting to their inanimate form? Did your brother wake up late, rush his breakfast before work, and leave without cleaning up? All these options are theoretically possible. But one of the four options is significantly more possible.

Abductive reasoning would tell us the answer is your brother's lateness. You don't have comprehensive proof, *but it is the explanation that best fits the observations you can make from the evidence in front of you.*

Abductive reasoning is forming an inference or a conclusion from the best evidence known. It is closely associated with induction. The difference is that induction is inferring from what is known and observed. Abductive reasoning is drawing a probable conclusion when you don't know everything. Philosopher Julian Baggini offers four criteria to work out whether an explanation is going to fly or not in an abductive sense:[17]

Simplicity. Is it the most straightforward explanation? Sure, it is possible a robber ate breakfast at your house and fed your cat, but the chance is vanishingly small. A friend who forgot to meet you for coffee might have started a vendetta against you, but they are more likely to just be careless and have forgotten. (Also, look at the later section on Occam's razor.)

Coherence. Does it fit with other facts that you know? In the case of the kitchen, you know your brother had an early shift, and you also know that he often runs a bit late. The mess will cohere with this explanation. If your brother was a neat freak and there had also been a small earthquake that morning, you might be okay with the remote possibility that it wasn't your brother leaving a mess.

Comprehensiveness. Does your theory take account of everything? If these are all the facts, then your brother's lateness is the most reliable explanation – it fits everything. The other theories would not have been comprehensive. In the case of the robber, why did he or she feed the cat? What does the case of the animate crockery say about our theories of consciousness and life on the planet?

Testability. A theory is better if you can test whether it is true. In this case you can ring your brother and say, 'Hey, did you leave the dishes out?' You cannot pick up the breakfast bowl and say, 'Hey, are you a cursed human destined to live as crockery?'

Let's apply the abductive test to the conspiracy theory that humans never landed on the moon, and the 'landing' was filmed in a studio lot in Los Angeles.

Firstly, is this theory simple? No, it is not. A conspiracy that would involve so many people who never went to the media and was covered up for over 50 years is hopelessly complicated and unlikely. One estimate is that 400,000 people would have had to stay quiet,[18] including the astronauts, author Arthur C. Clarke (who apparently wrote the script) and filmmaker Stanley Kubrick (who apparently filmed it). It would have been simpler to just go to the moon.

Secondly, is it coherent; does it fit with other facts we know? No. Many other facts and feats concerning space travel have emerged in the past 50 years showing the moon landing to be within the capabilities of technology and society. More recent hi-res photos of the moon show the flags that were planted there still standing.

Thirdly, is it comprehensive? Potentially, yes. Within its own conspiracy bubble it tells a complete story.

Fourthly, is it testable? No. We can't go and look at the studio lot where it was supposed to have been filmed. We can't interview the astronauts who say it was faked (because they don't say it was faked). We can't find a single positive piece of evidence to show that this enormous 'hoax' happened. All the 'evidence' offered by conspiracy theorists is criticism of the proof that there were people on the moon; for example, 'Why are there no stars in the pictures taken on the moon?' (answer: because it was daytime). Of course, conspiracy theorists can say that the lack of testable evidence points to how good the cover-up was, which takes us into the realm of the unfalsifiable theory.

In short, abduction is what we do each time we try to assess the available evidence to reach a reasonable conclusion. It's not foolproof but it works well in a practical, day-to-day way.

TRY IT OUT

What can you adduce from the following and why?

- You come home. There is a warm plate of spaghetti waiting for you. You have four flatmates, Ann, Bill, Cedric and Deidre. Ann is always out with her girlfriend at night. Bill is a gym junkie who never soils his body with carbohydrates. Cedric is a kind and generous assistant chef. Deidre is a mean-spirited person who would never think to make food for another person even if she was about to die of starvation.
- Drugs have been found in Jack's schoolbag. Three of Jack's friends claim he never takes drugs. Jack has given a speech to his class about why drugs are bad for you. Jack's older brother is a suspect character who was expelled from the school for drug trafficking. Jack has $100 in his wallet. The CCTV cameras at Jack's school broke down the previous week.

Conditional (if/then) reasoning

We will now move from the less formal 'inductive' and 'abductive' reasoning into more formal territory. (*Optional*: the next three pages are more head-scratchy than the rest of the book, so feel free to skip them.) We begin with conditional reasoning.

People use conditional reasoning every day without registering it: 'If I walk in the rain without an umbrella, then I will get wet'; 'If we double our sales, then our share price will go up'; 'If I cross the road in front of that truck, then I will get run over'. They are all statements that contain 'if/then'. You can see why it is called conditional reasoning – if the 'condition' in the first half of the sentence is met, then the second half of the sentence happens as well.

Half the time they work. Half the time they don't. Most of us have probably unconsciously worked out when they do and when they don't, but let's look at it properly. Being able to detect these in meetings, arguments and debates can be very handy. We will use examples as our starting point and work backwards.

Let's use the statement, 'If I come home after 10.00 pm I will use the back door of the house', and break it into four different modes.

Mode 1: Modus ponens (it's true!)

This is the easiest of the four.

Firstly, let's break the statement into a few lines:

> If I come home after 10.00 pm, I will use the back door of the house.
>
> I came home after 10.00 pm.
>
> So, I used the back door of the house.

If you want to get technical, you could reduce this argument to:

> If P (come home after 10.00 pm), then Q (use the back door of the house).
>
> P (came home after 10.00 pm).

So, Q (used the back door of the house).

No controversy here. If you are coming home late and don't want to wake the kids, your partner, your parents or the neighbours, you use the back door. You came home late one evening so you used the back door, just like you said.

Mode 2: Denying the antecedent (it's a fallacy!)

This is the dark shadow of modus ponens. Let's strip it down to its most basic form:

If P, then Q …

Not P so not Q.

The difference here is those 'nots'. Somehow, they have turned a true set of statements into a false set. Let's make it work with our example.

If I come home after 10.00 pm, I will use the back door of the house (if P, then Q).

I did not come home after 10.00 pm (not P).

So, I did not use the back door of the house (so not Q).

There are all sorts of reasons why you might use the back door of the house, not just because you are coming home late. Maybe it is closer to the garage, maybe you walked a different way home from the station, maybe you were parachuted into the back garden for kicks. Either way, you can't disprove the second half of the statement (you didn't use the back door) just because you disproved the first (you didn't come home late).

Mode 3: Modus tollens (it's true!)

We are now going to twist our late arrival home into another shape, with more Latin thrown in for good measure. Using our example:

If I come home after 10.00 pm, I will use the back door of the house (if P, then Q).

I did not use the back door of the house (not Q).

So, I did not come home after 10.00 pm (so not P).

This one is true too. If you stroll through the front door of the house, your family/friends/tenants/hostages can check their watches and know it will be before 10.00 pm. Easy.

Mode 4: Affirming the consequent (it's a fallacy!)

This one is the fallacious negative form of modus tollens. It's a bit misleading because it has a positive feel – there aren't any 'nots' in the statement and 'affirming' has a jolly, self-care ring to it. But don't be fooled – it's a fallacy.

> If P, then Q.
>
> Q then P.

Using our example:

> If I come home after 10.00 pm, I will use the back door of the house (if P then Q).
>
> I used the back door of the house (Q).
>
> So, I came home after 10.00 pm (so P).

In effect this is the same problem as denying the antecedent, just in a different form. I can use that back door any time I like, not just after 10.00 pm (when I must use it). I can use it in the morning, I can use it in the evening, I can use it at dawn or at the stroke of noon.

Affirming the consequent closes out other possible reasons that someone might take a particular action and leads to fallacious reasoning. For example, a trader might have a rule that if she thinks the options market will fall by 20 per cent in the next week, she will always sell half of her options to limit the damage. One day you see her sell half of her options. Do you sell your own options in a panic, thinking the market is about to dive? Not yet – there could be all sorts of reasons she has sold her options. She might be cashing in or see an opportunity elsewhere. You should not jump to conclusions using 'affirming the consequent'.

TRY IT OUT

Identify which mode (modus ponens, modus tollens, denying the antecedent, affirming the consequent) is at work in the following scenarios.

Scenario 1

A: If you go out in the woods today, you're sure of a big surprise

B: I did not go out in the woods today

C: I will not get a big surprise

Scenario 2

A: If you turn left at the bottom of the street you will run into Joe's Pizza House

B: I did not turn left at the bottom of the street

C: I did not run into Joe's Pizza's house

Scenario 3

A: If you put raw beef into a hot oven it will cook

B: I put my raw beef into a hot oven

C: My raw beef cooked

Scenario 4

A: If you read one more of these conditional reasoning exercises you will go mad

B: I went mad

C: I read one more of these conditional reasoning exercises

Answers

1. Denying the antecedent
2. Modens tollens
3. Modens ponens
4. Affirming the consequent

Deductive reasoning

Deductive reasoning is a particular type of reasoning that works in the realms of logic and analytical thinking. It essentially says that if you have correct premises and valid logical structures, then your conclusions will be sound. For example: 'All men are mortal, and Socrates is a man, therefore Socrates is mortal'. If the previous two sentences have got your heart racing in anticipation, then please go to the appendix for more thrilling details. If not, simply read on.

THE AC/DC METHOD OF JULIAN BAGGINI

It would be terrific if reasoning was like a sausage machine: present a problem, use a series of correct thinking procedures at the right time in the right way and watch the optimal answer come out the other side. Unfortunately, critical reasoning is less like a sausage machine and more like a minestrone soup. There are pieces of different shapes and sizes and indeterminate origin floating in the mix and no two bowls are exactly the same. Reasoning critically is messy and unpredictable, and it resists being reduced to an easy 'how to' list of steps.

This is partly why humans currently have an advantage over AI when it comes to thinking. We use the myriad elements of reasoning in different proportions and ways for each different situation as the need arises – we can be 'context specific'.

No one expects you to remember each element in this book, or to check each one off next time a thorny problem presents. But hopefully when situations do come up in real life, your memory will be jogged ('Should I buy this herbal remedy for my cold? Hang on, "regression to the mean" reminds me why I should not be persuaded').

Nonetheless, it would be good to take away a general approach that incorporates much of what we have looked at. Philosopher Julian Baggini, in his book *How to Think Like a Philosopher*,[19] suggests an 'AC/DC' model. It goes like this:

A is for 'attend'. Pay attention to what you are doing. *Attend.* Don't reason thoughtlessly. Keep concentrating and focusing, because it is not easy. Ask yourself if you are making assumptions, if you have biases, if you have argued properly using the proper steps, or if you are letting your ego get in the way. Have you paid enough attention to relevant facts? Have you used your ethical character as well as your logic? Are you being fair-minded? Be conscious about your thinking, instead of assuming you are already a hotshot at it. Consciousness isn't something AI is doing, and your restless and unprogrammed scanning of the reasoning environment to do the best thing possible will make you stronger.

C is for 'clarify'. Ask yourself what the problem really is. What are you really trying to solve? What do you want to achieve? Clarify what the relevant facts and pieces of evidence are. Scan the environment. Have you made the landscape clear enough? You can also look at how your argument is structured. What sort of argument is it?

D is for 'deconstruct'. This is deeper than just 'analyse'. It means taking the argument apart before putting it back together again. Does your argument proceed properly? Have you made the right distinctions where you needed to? Have you been biased in how you have collected your facts? Are some of the facts weak or just distractions? Is your personality and character getting in the way – are you coming up with an argument just to justify your emotions, ego or attitudes? Did you get rid of something that was true or important just because you didn't like the look of it?

C is for 'connect'. After breaking it down, it's time to both put your argument back together and look around even more. What does your argument and decision look like in its entirety? How does it compare with other arguments or decisions out there? Are there insights from other areas that seem unconnected but could add value to your argument? Have you put the logical, the emotional, the psychological and the possibility of bias all together? Can you call your thinking fair-minded?

This is more of an approach than a set of procedures. But if you take AC/DC into your reasoning you will probably be one of the most careful and thorough thinkers in the room.

CHAPTER 2

EVERYDAY THINKING ABOUT THE WORLD

This section focuses on the information you consume about the world around you. Some civic debates are about issues: should we have more or less immigration, should we lower taxes, should we phase out fossil fuels more quickly? Holding considered views about these issues is part of being a citizen. Other questions asked in the public sphere tend to focus on 'what really happened': what led to the replacement of the prime minister, what did the energy company know before the oil spill, was that election fair?

There have always been vexed areas in the public arena. But they are now vexed in new ways. In the distant past there was a barely a trickle of information available. Before the printing press, people had to rely on fifth-hand accounts from others. It was generally futile. Imagine yourself as a medieval villager in Norfolk attempting to work out the civic temperature in the distant city of London. What a traveller – and there weren't many – heard from another traveller, who heard it from a farrier, who was having a drink with a man at the pub 30 miles from London … well, that was about as good as you were going to get.

Print newspapers (and reading) released the tap of information. Anyone who bought a newspaper or received a pamphlet could read second-hand what was happening in the towns and cities of their country. Journalists could investigate what was happening and include their opinions. This came with the issue of who controlled the tap. Media barons for centuries have had enormous power to shape information and views. If a government gained control of the newspapers (as regularly happened in fascist and communist states in the twentieth century), they were able to indoctrinate whole populations.

In liberal societies, though, the flow of information and views steadily increased. There were multiple newspapers with different views and multiple television stations with different approaches. Magazines and journals abounded. There was more information and opinion than could reasonably be handled – but it was also controlled by the industry of journalism (and delivered to you once a day or week, not once every few minutes).

Then came the internet. The tap broke and the geyser opened. Any view, however wild, could find a home. The rosy view was that this democratised information. The thorny view was that this horizontalisation of information meant the rantings of tech savvy, but crazy, cousin Merv could look as polished and real as a Pulitzer Prize-winning journalist from *The New York Times*. And there was so, so much of it. Its frequency also increased. Twenty-four-hour news stations delivered updates and stories by the hour instead of by the day. More news and views were needed to fill this relentless cycle.

Then came social media. The geyser became a flood. You could get a steady diet of Pulitzer Prize-winning journalists or a steady diet of crazy cousin Merv every day, every hour. You could link with established journalists, experts and thought leaders or, if you preferred, all crazy cousin Merv's crackpot friends. You could curate your news so you only heard varieties of what you agreed with. People could find themselves in political echo chambers much more easily.

Then the 'weaponisation' (ie the use to create deliberate harm) of information became more refined. Bad actors, often from other nations, could create false stories that looked convincing and pour them into the social media flood with the purpose of destabilising the public sphere. Technology, particularly AI, allows bad actors to create not just text, but voices and images indistinguishable from reality. Others found that more extreme views result in more clicks, traffic and monetisation, motivating them to become more one-sided and angrier. Extremism has been commodified.

So, here we are in the second quarter of the twenty-first century. We know we are not telling you anything you don't know already. However, it means critical thinking and critical discernment about public affairs is needed more than ever. Individually, we might not have much influence on the world, but each of us can commit to using critical thinking and practised rationality when judging, assessing, changing our minds and advocating points of view.

The thinking we use to make decisions and the thinking we use to consider public affairs are treated as separate chapters in this handbook, but they overlap substantially. Hopefully what you read will help you both navigate the public arena and make clearer decisions.

TRUTH

Theories of truth

The *Oxford English Dictionary* states that truth is 'a statement or an account which is accordance with the facts'.[20] As Aristotle would say, the truth corresponds with what is. This is why so much hinges on what is a 'fact' (see below).

The truth can also 'state what is the case'. This can include statements that are 'true' by being logically sound, such as 'Bob is younger than his parents'; 'Parallel lines never cross'; 'If Jeremy is shorter than Chris and Chris is shorter than Cindy, then Jeremy is shorter than Cindy'. These are also known as deductive statements – and as previously promised there is much more about them in the appendix to this book. These true statements tend not to be controversial, and you will not find yourself embroiled in many arguments about them unless you are in very contrarian company.

There can also be inductive truths about the future: 'The sun rose the day before yesterday, the sun rose yesterday and so the sun is going to rise tomorrow'. Now the sun is very, very, very probably going to rise tomorrow – but it's not a done deal. The sun might blow up later this afternoon or be vaporised by a passing intergalactic fleet consumed by malice. However, this prospect is vanishingly small. 'The sun will rise tomorrow' passes the threshold of a truth due to its extraordinary likelihood.

Truth is also linked with objectivity and a capacity to be able to demonstrate a fact over and over again. 'There is a drink in the fridge' (keep opening the fridge); 'Jo Fudge works as a railway ticket inspector' (go check the ticket office); 'Fanta is orange' (pour it out). A series of factual truths can also be used to assemble an inductive conclusion that is also securely true: 'Dad stocks the fridge with Fanta', 'The railway employs ticket officers to check tickets'.

Truth can also extend to facts that you can verify through research, even if you do not have personal experience of them. This links to 'evidence': 'Botswana in a country in Africa'; 'The temperature of dry ice is –109 degrees Fahrenheit'; 'Benjamin Disraeli was the British prime minister between 1874 and 1880'.

There are three different theories of truth:

The correspondence theory of truth – it accurately reports the way the world really is (eg how weather works).

The coherence theory of truth – it fits in with other ideas or statements (eg statements about Euclidean geometry, or the theory of relativity).

The pragmatic theory of truth – beliefs which are useful or have a practical application.

Why truth is contested

If truth can be so soberly described and defined, even if not completely agreed upon, why has it always been such a contested political issue? And if we agree with a common view that this issue is getting more intense, why?

One reason is that some people call their subjective opinions 'truth' to make them appear stronger: 'Abortion is wrong, no two ways about it'; 'John is a jerk, that's just the truth'.

A second reason is the dissemination of manufactured false facts. These can combine to create a 'truth' narrative that is not true. The recent advent of fake news and technologically altered evidence adds a dangerous contemporary twist to this (more on this later).

Thirdly, many people increasingly talk about truth itself in subjective terms: 'You have your truth, I have mine' or 'That is just my truth'. People might speak about the 'truth' of their feelings, but this is so obvious (people's internal feelings are not false) as to be tautological. This in turn makes the word 'truth' hollow. You cannot create an objective truth about what you feel.

On one hand, it is fitting to say the two parties in most divorces have different experiences and different ways of seeing events that should both be respected. This does not mean there are two different truths. Both parties lived in a shared physical reality. 'Truth' is cleaner when it can be kept to situations and phenomena that can be verified.

Objective territory	**Subjective territory**
Truth	Argument
Fact	View
Knowledge	Opinion
Accuracy	Judgement
Proof	Belief
	Evaluation

TRY IT OUT

Can these statements be true, and in what ways?

- My uncle and aunt's divorce wasn't really anyone's fault.
- The angles in a triangle add up to 180 degrees.
- Kellie Smith works as a real estate agent in Sydney.
- It is the woman's right to choose to terminate a pregnancy.
- In my mental truth, everybody I meet likes me.
- The earth's climate is heating up at least partly because of human activity.
- You feel more comfortable when you own your own home.
- Broccoli is good for your health.

Facts

The issue of 'facts' has jumped out of primary school classrooms to increasingly dominate our democracies and our society. Facts are the building blocks of our judgements, our opinions and our decisions. Recently they have become even more of an arena of debate themselves, instead of the neutral, agreed-upon data on which we build our arguments. The shakiness of what a 'fact' is can be seen as a fundamental threat to civic liberal democracies, so it is important to be clear-headed about what facts are.

Let's start with a definition from the *Cambridge Dictionary*, which defines a fact as 'something that is known to have happened or to exist, especially something for which proof exists, or about which there is information'.[21]

A fact is based on what we know, not what we believe.

Facts are 'inductive'. They rely on some combination of experience and memory. For example, 'That is a chair in front of you' can be considered a fact as you can see the chair in front of you. 'I fell over yesterday' is a fact you can remember. 'Your friend Paul lives at 22 Arbour Drive' is a fact because you have visited Paul there several times. These facts are uncontroversial. There are other facts backed by proof that can be easily verified. Mark Ella was the captain of the Wallabies rugby team in 1982. The French Revolution began in 1789. Water boils at 100 degrees Celsius at sea level.

We could end the explanation of facts right there and go forward with this crisp understanding. However, it would not explain the contemporary crisis about the nature of facts in our public discourse. So, let's press on.

Philosopher, scientist and mathematician René Descartes did some (necessary) damage to the notion of a 100 per cent, rolled-gold fact. He suggested that even though we think we can see, hear and touch things, we might actually be trapped in an 'experience machine' run by an evil demon. This demon has you wired up and is sending you false impressions of everything you are seeing, touching and hearing. The more common version of this is 'right now you might actually be in a dream'.

Let's try it.

You think you are sitting on a chair right now? That's just the evil demon pumping that message to the touch sensors of your brain. You think your partner is stacking the dishwasher in the next room? That's the evil demon pumping fake memories of your partner – s/he doesn't even exist. You think you are you? You are actually a 98-year-old woman trapped inside an experience machine being pumped false memories of an individual you think of as you.

You can't absolutely disprove any of this (people have spent centuries trying and no one has managed it), which means there is no such thing as a rolled-gold, 100 per cent fact. This is 'epistemology (the theory of knowledge) 101', a fundamental and very interesting branch of philosophy. You could spend your whole life exploring its depths. However, we will move on to something we can consider in our everyday civic life.

So, nothing can be absolutely, undeniably proved to a rolled-gold total 100 per cent standard. There is always the tiniest sliver of doubt. But that doesn't mean people should be able to drive in a truck full of lies, falsehoods and craziness into that sliver of doubt. As Julian Baggini says in *How to Think Like a Philosopher*, 'It is easy to slide from the justified belief that nothing can be known for certain to the deeply sceptical conclusion that nothing is really known at all. Some find this thrilling. But it is also toxic since it leaves us with no reason to believe anything and so no basis upon which to act.'[22]

For argument's sake, let's say the 'fact' that you are reading this book is really just 99.99 per cent fact. That's good enough, isn't it? You can presume it is true enough. Look up at the ceiling. What colour is the ceiling? Whatever it is, you can presume that to be about 99.99 per cent true (after all, you could be colour blind and just not know it). But really, the colour you said is good enough to get on with. What about 'Laos is a country in Asia'? You might not have been to Laos, but it's in endless books, many people have reported going there and you could buy a ticket to go there. Shall we call it 99.99 per cent? Again, good enough to accept.

But come down just a couple of micro-fractions of a per cent and you enter the world of the strange conspiracy theorists who try to play havoc with accepted facts. Is the Earth spherical? Yes, it is. But hang on, it looks flat from where I am standing. Everyone used to believe it was flat. There are websites out there saying the Earth is flat. They explain the Earth is a disc with the icecaps all around the side. Science itself accepts that any theory could be disproved one day by a better theory. So maybe the earth being spherical is just a 99.99 per cent fact. Rather than getting tied up in knots trying to get a spherical Earth to 100 per cent we should take our chances and assume the Earth is actually spherical.

And so it goes on. Is there a Bigfoot monster in the woods behind your house? Is climate change just a hoax run by the United Nations to start a world government? Into these tiny, tiny, tiny slivers of existential doubt, some people can wedge open a chasm in their brains then pour in bunkum to which they give credence. Because after all, it *just might* be true.

But we need to calm down.

Even at 99.99 per cent, facts are solid. It is unreasonable, impossible even, to expect them to jump the vast gulf between 99.99 per cent and 100 per cent. On facts, and with facts, you can build your decisions, create your world view and construct your opinions. But they stand independent from you. They are true, whether you like it or not. You have to find the relevant facts, but you can't just make them up because they fit the opinion you want. As the US politician Daniel Moynihan said so pithily in 1983, 'Everyone is entitled to his own opinion, but not to his own facts'.

So, having come down from a 100 per cent fact to 99.99 per cent, let's now go the other way. Let's build a 'fact' up from zero to 99 per cent – or at least something close.

Let's start with 'Joe steals meat pies'. Just saying it does not make it true. It is an assertion or an allegation only. It hovers at just a tiny fraction of a per cent true, because most people do not steal meat pies. I could say it more loudly: 'JOE STEALS MEAT PIES'. I could say it frequently: 'Joe steals meat pies, Joe steals meat pies, Joe steals meat pies, Joe steals meat pies'. I could make up a plausible fantasy narrative about how Joe steals meat pies to impress the ladies down at the sausage roll emporium. I could pay off my friends to tell you Joe steals meat pies. I could buy a TV station and get the opinion editors to say Joe steals meat pies. I could run a business and make my workers' employment dependent on swearing that Joe steals meat pies. I could get members of parliament to say there have been concerning allegations that Joe steals meat pies. However, it hasn't become any more true (even though you may suspect Joe steals meat pies more than you did at the beginning of this paragraph). It is still just an assertion.

Something becomes a fact when a statement is backed up with evidence. There is another section in this chapter about amassing evidence, but for the moment, using Joe as our example, we would perhaps:

- get witness statements from people who say they saw Joe steal pies
- get security camera footage showing Joe stealing pies
- get Joe to admit it
- find a criminal record of Joe stealing pies.

Any one of these pieces of supporting evidence would shoot 'Joe steals meat pies' up to 80, 90, even 95 per cent reliable. In combination they would go further, perhaps into the very high 90s. If people saw Joe steal pies, the camera filmed it, he 'fessed up to it and he'd been let out of jail the day before for stealing pies, then we'd have a pretty clear fact that Joe steals meat pies … at least factual enough to accept.

TRY IT OUT

How do these rate as facts, and why?

- World War I happened.
- The Battle of Bergerac happened in 1345.
- Vaccinations help prevent the spread of coronavirus.
- Your mother was a woman.
- Your mother is a woman.
- Nuclear reactors are generally safe.
- New Delhi is the capital of India.
- Humans evolved from more simple animals.

Opinions

According to the *Cambridge Dictionary*, an opinion is 'a thought or belief about something or someone/the thoughts or beliefs that a group of people have/a judgment about someone or something'.[23] While a fact is based on what we know, an opinion is based on what we believe. I know who the prime minister is, and I believe he/she is doing a good job. An opinion is always inconclusive. Often, when we support our opinion with facts and data, it can become an argument or a judgement. Both are stronger, but not as 'true' as a fact.

The gulf between an opinion and a fact is a key distinction in public discourse. Mixing them can muddy our own thinking, and that of others. When someone says, 'Jane Doe has a secret mission to destroy healthcare if she gets into government and that's a fact', they are mixing up fact and opinion. When someone says, 'People claim Jane Doe cut $200 million out of the healthcare budget last time she was in government, but that's just their opinion', they are also mixing up fact and opinion, just the other way around.

Opinions might include: 'The Matildas are a great football team' or 'Smoking and stress caused my stomach cancer' or 'Solar panels should be used widely on houses'. All debatable, all contingent – and all much more solid if built on a bedrock of solid, verifiable facts.

Although they can be very well justified, opinions cannot ever be completely proven. Whether it is wise for your firm to expand into a new market or make a new product will always be a matter of opinion (even after the results come in). What house you should buy will never be satisfied to a factual level. What political party you should vote for at the next election will always be a matter of your own judgement and world view. There is always an irreducible degree of judgement and contestability in an opinion which means it will never be a fact. (Tip – if a question has 'should' in it, then it is almost always a matter of opinion.)

You can break opinions into three different types.

The first is an **opinion of preference**. This is an opinion about matters of taste. Some of us prefer strawberry ice-cream, some vanilla and some chocolate. You could survey millions of people, you could mount advertising campaigns, you could offer Neapolitan ice-cream tubs to every family in the country to see which stripe of flavour is left icing up in the freezer. But you wouldn't get closer to which flavour was better because it is just a matter of preference. So too is what colour to paint a room (unless you choose brown, which is objectively bad), or whether to visit London or Paris. We can have diverting discussions about these things, but no one needs to get hot under the collar.

The second is an **opinion of evaluation**. This is the most common type of opinion. It is an opinion where you have weighed up evidence, looked at the issues and come up with a reasoned position. But someone else could still have a different reasonable opinion. Most elections come down to this. Many people will sift through the policies of the government, judge its performance and re-elect it. Many others will consider and evaluate the same policies, compare them with the alternatives and vote for the opposition. However reasonable and well thought out a decision is, it is still a result of an evaluative opinion. Many issues – nuclear power versus solar power, immigration levels, funding for hospitals or defence etc, etc, etc – are opinions of evaluation.

A third type of opinion is an **opinion about a fact**. This is an opinion about the truth of an 'objective' statement, such as an event or a phenomenon. You can have an opinion about whether violent crime is down in your neighbourhood or not, but there will be an objective, statistical fact about it. You can have an opinion about whether there is life elsewhere in the universe, but either there is or there isn't.

For a more detailed example, let's look at one of the world's most famous criminal cases, that of Australian mother Lindy Chamberlain, who was charged with killing her 10-week-old baby Azaria at a camping site near Uluru in 1980 and always maintained the baby was taken by a dingo. There were many strong views and opinions at the time. People were transfixed by every piece of evidence, expert testimony and witness statements, Lindy's religion, rust patterns in her car and whether they were foetal haemoglobin, and more. Opinions were incredibly strongly held. But these opinions didn't in any way affect the truth or the fact of the matter. Either Lindy Chamberlain killed her baby that night or she did not. There was a factual truth out there; it was just hard to discern. When the facts are in dispute, it doesn't mean there are no facts; just that they are in dispute. (For the record, Lindy Chamberlain did not kill her baby. Overwhelming evidence in the form of Azaria's clothing, which was discovered several years later at the base of Uluru, confirmed a dingo had taken her.) Another way of describing opinions about matters of fact is to call them 'true beliefs' or 'false beliefs'.[24]

Opinions about facts can be quite well considered and judged, even if they are false, because the person forming the opinion might have been fed misleading or wrong facts. Philosophy professor Christoffer Lammer-Heindel in *Philosophy Now*[25] uses the example of a child who believes in Santa Claus because their parents have created sleigh marks in the grass, chewed on a carrot left out on Christmas Eve and consumed the Christmas rum left near the chimney. The child will have a well-formed opinion – indeed judgement – that Santa is real. But it will be a false one. There are multiple examples of this in current affairs.

Admittedly, these categories can be blurry. Is your favourite football team (which is on the top of the table) 'better' than your brother's (which is on the bottom)? There are elements of preference, evaluation and fact in this. So too in preferring the music of Beethoven to that of DJ Khaled. In deciding on facts such as those in a murder trial you also need to 'evaluate' evidence.

Yet identifying the different types of opinion can also create clarity. This can be seen in the climate debate of recent decades, with its often furious discourse about how much climate change is the result of human activity. Endless editorials, opinion pieces, speculation about motives, and calls for journalistic 'balance' (requiring as many 'anti' points of view as 'pro') have proliferated. So much of the debate has been treated as an opinion of evaluation – like an election, where all our views count and we all get to individually make up our minds. But it's not an election or something that can be decided through a majority opinion. It's an opinion about a fact. Either the world's climate is heating at least partially because of human activity, or it isn't. The climate isn't sitting around waiting to see what we decide about whether it is heating up. It's just heating up. Our misrecognition of the nature of the climate debate as 'evaluative' rather than opinion about a fact (or true versus false belief) could go down as the worst mistake the human species has ever made.

TRY IT OUT

Are these opinions? If they are, which type are they most like?

- Sushi tastes great.
- Nuclear reactors are generally safe.
- Aeroplanes are the safest form of travel.
- The Labor Party are good economic managers.
- The Liberal Party are good at running education.
- The Sydney Swans are the best AFL team.
- It is better to invest in the share market than in property.
- We should not eat meat.

EVIDENCE

As we have seen, if you want to make a claim about something other than your feelings or preferences, you should find evidence for it. The *Cambridge Dictionary* defines evidence as: 'acts, information, documents etc that give reason to believe that something is true'.[26]

The last decade has made this more difficult. There is now a lot of credible-looking detritus online. There is also a lot of *in*credible looking detritus that some people adhere to regardless. It makes the ability to discern and sort the type, quality and veracity of evidence more crucial.

Categories of evidence

So, what are the different categories of evidence, good and bad? Philosopher Robert Arp outlines them.[27]

Firstly, there is **direct sense evidence of spatiotemporal entities**. Sense evidence is sight, hearing, touch, etc. A spatiotemporal entity is … well … a thing. A good example of this is being able to prove that the coffee shop up the road exists. You go there, you see the waiter, you touch the menu, you drink the coffee. Yes, it is definitely there.

Secondly, there is **sense evidence of spatiotemporal entities that is indirect through a device**. Let's say the Shalimar Gardens in Kashmir, India exist. You have probably never been there. But you can look at photos of them on the internet. You can look at videos of them. You can read about them. You can be sufficiently convinced that they are really there. This also includes objects that can be discerned only through a device. There are stars you can't see with your naked eye, but you can see them if you point a telescope in their direction. There are cells you can't see with your naked eye that can be seen under a microscope.

Thirdly, there is the **testimony of others whom we trust**. What are the symptoms of the new bird flu virus? Your niece Jane has had it. She reports having the mildest sore throat and nothing more. So, it is true that a symptom of the bird flu virus can be the mildest of sore throats. At the same time, your Uncle Jim had it. He reported a terrible inability to breathe, fever and muscle pain. So, these are also the symptoms of bird flu virus. Based on testimony of those you trust, bird flu has a host of different symptoms.

Fourthly, there is the **testimony of experts in some area, domain or discipline**. You want to buy the coffee shop up the road and you want to see if it is structurally sound. You get a structural engineer to help you, and he says the joists are dodgy, the materials are weak and the place could well collapse in the next decade. It looks fine to you. But the engineer is an expert, and you should trust him over your own sense data.

Fifthly, there are **authoritative explanations from the sciences**. The sciences tell you that sufficiently tested vaccinations for tetanus and measles are safe. This is good evidence and should be enough to give you confidence in them. Uncle Jim, a real estate agent, might tell you that vaccinations for tetanus and measles are a scam, but trusting his real estate advice would not be evidence enough for you to believe him on this issue. In addition, we can trust science when it tells you how gravity or electricity works.

Last, there are **logical or mathematical explanations**. These are deductive explanations. For example, if you are in the Shalimar Gardens and the Shalimar Gardens are in India, then it is logically true that you are in India.

The world of legal reasoning also provides a different set of helpful distinctions in sorting and sifting evidence.

There is the difference between **direct and circumstantial evidence**. Direct evidence is a witness or a document that can clearly prove a claim.[28] Want to know whether Jane stabbed Joe? If Bill says, 'Yes, I saw Jane put a knife in Joe's chest' then you have your direct evidence. Want to know whether Jane took out a million-dollar loan using the company's money? Produce the document showing the loan for a million dollars in her name and you have your direct evidence. Of course, you have to be a little careful that Bill is actually telling the truth, and the document is not a forgery, but broadly, direct evidence is the gold standard.

Circumstantial evidence is when someone provides proof of a different fact that can lead to a deduction about the claim in question.[29] Want to know whether Jane stabbed Joe? If Bill says, 'Yes, I saw Jane go into the room with Joe, and I heard them argue, then Joe started screaming', this is circumstantial evidence. It might have been Jane who stabbed Joe, or it might have been an intruder who broke in on them both while they were arguing. Want to know whether Jane took out a million-dollar loan using the company's money? Produce a document showing that Jane was a million dollars in debt for gambling and you have circumstantial evidence showing motive, but nothing more.

Another distinction is **original and hearsay evidence**. Original evidence is when a person can say they saw something themselves. Hearsay (or reported) evidence is where someone is relying on what a third person said. Want to know whether Jane stabbed Joe? If Bill says, 'Yes, I saw Jane stab Joe in the chest', you have your original evidence. If Bill says, 'I was speaking to the cleaner, who was chatting to the plumber who bumped into the flower courier who said they saw Jane stab Joe', then you have hearsay evidence only. It's still a pretty good lead, but you should have a chat to the flower courier instead of relying on Bill.[30]

TRY IT OUT

What sort of evidence would you rely on to decide the truth or falsity of these claims?

- There are islands to the north of Norway called Svalbard.
- There is a Woolworths shopping centre near our house.
- It is very bad when you have a migraine.
- Flying is the safest form of motorised travel.
- Vaccinations are a good way to lower the risk of severe flu.
- The Labor Party won the 2025 federal election in Australia.
- Our universe started in the Big Bang approximately 13.7 billion years ago.
- 2+2=4.

Standards and burden of proof

People are asked to prove their arguments all the time. It can happen in the public sphere or in our workplaces. This is fair enough: we should expect proof and evidence from others, and they are entitled to expect it from us.

When we need to prove something there is a matter of degrees. At one end of the spectrum someone could say, 'Mars is made of blue cheese – prove me wrong', thereby holding themself to practically a zero per cent proof threshold. On the other hand, someone at a dinner party could say, 'I'm not convinced this blue cheese in front of me is in fact blue cheese, because I might just be in a dream'. For this person, all the evidence of their senses that there is a piece of blue cheese in front of them is not enough. They are looking for a proof percentage that is just unattainable.

In short, it is just about impossible to ever totally prove or disprove something. Instead, we should determine a reasonable standard of proof between zero per cent and 100 per cent depending on the situation. The law has been helpful in coming up with some standards that can also help make decisions and come to conclusions in everyday life.

Let's use the example of 'our costs accountant Chris might be embezzling company funds'. It's your job to decide whether he is, then to act.

Sitting in the middle of standard of proof is **balance of probabilities**. This means 50 per cent plus one. If, based on all the evidence, you judge it more likely than not that Chris is embezzling company funds, you can say it happened on the balance of probabilities. This is the standard used most of the time in cases that aren't criminal cases. Courts use this standard because if it was much higher, unscrupulous people would get away with illegal acts all the time. But be careful with balance of probabilities. There is still a good chance Chris is not embezzling funds – up to 40 or 45 per cent in fact. Society wouldn't want to send someone to jail for serious embezzlement if there was a 40 per cent chance they didn't do it.

This is why a much higher standard is frequently used: **beyond reasonable doubt**. It is the standard used in criminal trials, and it means you have to be extremely confident indeed. If you have a well-founded ('reasonable') doubt about any aspect of the event or case, it can't be said to have been proven. This does not mean you have to prove it 100 per cent. Imagine that six independent employees testify that they knew Chris had embezzled company funds, the holes in the accounts are there to see, and Chris's personal account balance mysteriously goes up each month by the same amount that the company's accounts go down. It would not be good enough for Chris to claim that George the CFO had it in for him, bribed the six employees, cooked the company accounts and transferred the money into Chris's account. That might provide a fanciful doubt. But it does not provide a reasonable doubt. It is overwhelmingly more likely that Chris is making the whole conspiracy theory up. Chris would have embezzled the accounts beyond reasonable doubt.

However, as a decision maker in the company, these two standards of proof are not hugely helpful. The balance of probabilities is too low. Taking action against Chris on only a 51 per cent probability could easily expose you to employment law trouble – and it also means there is an enormous chance you've taken action against an innocent person. On the other hand, beyond reasonable doubt is too high. If you had to wait for a criminal standard of proof before you could reprimand or dismiss Chris, you would be waiting a long time and Chris would very probably continue to defraud you in the interim.

This is why there are burdens of proof between these two that you might find more useful in making a decision or a judgement.

One is **clear and convincing evidence**. This is evidence that is much more probably true than false. It would be reasonable to dismiss Chris if you found the evidence to be both convincing and apparent. Schools could use this to discipline or suspend a child and parents could use this to send a child to their room. There are a variety of other 'burdens', many of them used in US courts. These include 'reasonable to believe', 'preponderance of evidence' and 'probable cause'. All require varieties of clear and unambiguous evidence.

On the other hand, there are levels of proof below balance of probabilities. One is **reasonably plausible**. This lower standard is useful if it is important for a person to be believed and there is no chance of injustice to someone else. Others at this end of the burden of proof rainbow include 'some evidence', 'some credible evidence', 'reasonable indications' and 'reasonable suspicion'.

With any argument or decision, it's important to determine which side has the burden of proof. That side needs to make stronger arguments to be believed. For example, should you buy new tyres to replace balding ones or let them go another year? The potential cost of not buying new tyres is so great that the burden lies on the side of the argument saying, 'Put it off'.[31] Similarly, someone saying, 'The accounts department is defrauding the company' should shoulder the burden of proof.

All in all, when asked to 'prove' or 'believe' something, you have to make a call about what standard is appropriate. It's all shades of grey. If you make it zero per cent or 100 per cent you are on a short road to believing everything … or nothing at all.

TRY IT OUT

Who has the burden of proof here? What standard should be used in each case?

- Marcel killed Marceau with a knife.
- This new blend of vitamin A, B and K will do wonders for your anxiety and stress.
- I think the woman in the next office is logging into my profile when I go to lunch.
- This new company looks like a good investment, and I will invest one-tenth of my savings in it.
- I'd like to take a job at that new construction company because the conditions are good, but I suspect they are a bit shonky.
- That new Italian pizza place looks good – let's try it.

Credibility and relying on experts

One way to amass evidence to support or challenge a view is relying on experts. This does not mean complete reliance. AI-generated opinions are becoming more ubiquitous. The horizontality of social media platforms allows more people to purport to be experts without having to pass through the more traditional gatekeepers – publishers, newspapers or television stations. This might be democratising, but it also elevates people with only a basement, a microphone and a God complex.

And the threat to the public sphere is more significant than that. There is a newfound respect for some online opinion makers precisely because they have no expertise. Knowing about your subject area can see you derided as an elite. Scientists who know what they are talking about are trolled precisely because they know what they are talking about.

But it's worse than that too. The proliferation of weaponised fake facts makes it more important that credible, trusted experts exist to shape our news and views and filter out what is fake. Sadly, this is happening even as these experts are harder to find, and their credibility is questioned.

All of this means we need to be able to assess experts and rely on them more than ever. A checklist to assess the claims of an expert might include:

- their **education**.[32] Education in their claimed area of expertise is a major factor. Also, where did they get their qualifications? Some institutions are rigorous; others are fraudulent mail order houses.
- **recognition** as an expert in their field. This will often be because they are an academic. If they are at a reputable university, all the better. They could also be a senior person at a relevant firm – a partner at a law firm, a doctor at a teaching hospital,

or a traffic management expert at an urban regulation advisory company.

- **experience**. As a rule of thumb, 30 years is better than three months. On the other hand, beware of people who have not kept up to date.
- **advising** in their area of expertise. A mergers and acquisitions lawyer doesn't necessarily have much to say about criminal law or traffic management. An academic with expertise in thirteenth-century Europe won't have much to tell us about the situation in China. People can have valuable information outside their area of specialisation and training, though a cancer doctor talking about nutrition could still be worth listening to.
- **first-hand knowledge** of the area they are talking about.
- their **reputation**, along with which people value that reputation. A GP might be considered a medical expert among her teacher friends about various cancers, but that doesn't mean she is so qualified that she should advise the government on cancer prevention policy.
- **motivation**. Are they being paid to offer a view – and by whom? Expert witnesses appear in court cases, but they are often being paid by one side or another. This doesn't make their evidence useless, but it is worth keeping in mind. Sometimes whole research careers are funded by companies to get a particular result that looks respectable. A number of books about diets have been written by doctors who know that the better their particular diet sounds, the more copies they will sell. The more the authors of critical thinking books indicate that you can get smarter just by reading a book, the more copies it will sell … hang on, that's just our *inside* voice, right?

It is also worth asking whether an expert is offering their expertise about a matter of fact (for example, how many car parking spots you need in your proposed shopping centre to comply with local council regulations) or a matter of evaluation, such as whether people should own guns. If it is a matter of evaluation there is still a lot of scope for your own consideration.

It is near impossible to get rolled-gold reliability from an expert. At some point, we do have to trust people. We trust car mechanics to fix our cars, for example. They seem to run a reputable place, they are helpful, what they say seems to make sense in our limited experience about cars, the cars tend to run better after they have worked on them, and other people have made lots of good comments about their repair shop on social media. We could still be wrong. It is not completely impossible that the regulator will close them down for shoddy workmanship in a year or two. But judicious trust is needed to be able to get on in the world.[33]

Sources of information

While we're on the topic of expertise, let's consider different sources of information. Sources are what the experts (or not) use to support their views. They include books, talks, videos, articles, websites and so on. There are reliable and not-so-reliable versions of each of these. Consider:

- How reputable is the publisher? Is it the BBC (good) or the publishing arm of the Ku Klux Klan (not so good)? Does the publisher have their own barrow to push, or are they interested in a variety of views?
- Does it quote and use other reputable sources for corroboration? That's good – but watch out for 'groupthink', which happens when academics or publishers all jump on a bandwagon.[34] You should also watch out for dubious sources that footnote a number of other dubious sources to look more authoritative (it can be a frustrating footnoting hall of mirrors).
- Is the source anonymous? Websites can often be, in effect, anonymous. Be careful about using a website or platform from a source you don't otherwise recognise (*Stanford Encyclopaedia of Philosophy* is probably good, *Philozophy for da Boyz* might not be so good).
- How big is the claim being made? The claim that prolonged exposure to sunlight can cause skin cancer is pretty well established. But if the claim is that eating goji berries is the cure for skin cancer, the source should be unimpeachable. In fact, you should expect a reliable source and a great deal of corroboration.
- When was it written? Is it out of date?

TRY IT OUT

Out of 10, how much would you trust each of these people or organisations? Why?

- Sibyl Spike, the Head of the World Medical Association, says vaccinations are vital to stop the spread of coronavirus.
- Sibyl Spike, the Head of the World Medical Association, says everyone staying in their house for a year is vital to allow them to recharge from the fast pace of modern life.
- Finn Kerflups, a Masters student in Economics, tells the media that we are about to go into a recession.
- Finn Kerflups, a Masters student in Economics, tells his family Christmas gathering that we are about to go into a recession.
- Brandy McSlurry, a fashion influencer, says shoes should be flat.
- Brandy McSlurry, a fashion influencer, says the world is flat.
- Bear Dawson, Professor of Lung Diseases at Oxford New University, says smoking vapes is only half as harmful as cigarettes in a study subsidised by Vapes R Us.
- Phillandra Flake, a mother of two, writes a bestselling book called *Budgeting and Home Maintenance for Busy Mums.*

PERILS AND PRECAUTIONS

Navigating generalisations

Mostly we should pillory generalisations, call them out, and take them out to the garbage like the insipid, weaselly purveyors of prejudice and sloppy thinking they are. But before that, a word or two in their defence.

Generalisations help us make reasonable decisions about the world. For example, if you travel on four different reputable international airlines and find you get a fairly comfortable but small seat, some decent entertainment and a passable meal, then travel on a fifth reputable international airline, you can be reasonably confident it will have a comfortable but small seat, some decent entertainment and a passable meal. You have generalised your experience so you don't have to do all the research about what you will get on this fifth carrier.

We generalise all the time: how many kids your child will have in their class; whether California will vote Democrat at the next US election; what food sits together in the aisles of different supermarkets. It is a good mental shortcut. And it is a key part of inductive thinking.

Generalisations go wrong when you apply to every member of a group characteristics that only in fact belong to some members of the group ('Tables have four legs'; 'Italians have moustaches'). The problem is the submerged 'all' at the beginning of generalised sentences. If you say, for example, 'deep down, people just want to be understood', what you are really saying is all people just want to be understood deep down. Actually, some people couldn't give a damn whether others understand them deep down or not. When you say 'people at my work are psychopaths', you are consigning them all to the psychopathic bucket.

This can create prejudice and reproduce a lack of nuance, both of which are bad for critical thinking and decision making. Generalisations are generally the root cause of stereotypes and prejudice: 'Australians are loud'; 'British people are reserved'; 'Scandinavians like their IKEA'. They also can push you towards less subtle solutions; for example, 'people like to be greeted as they walk into a shop – so greet everyone when they walk in' (actually not everyone likes it), or 'lawyers make a lot of money, so I'll train to be a lawyer' (lots of graduates will be bitterly disappointed).

As philosopher Philip Cam points out, there are a few ways to undo a bad generalisation. The first is to find counterexamples. It's very hard to say 'all swans are white' when someone can take you to the zoo and point out a black swan. It is hard to insist all lawyers make a lot of money when you can point to a few who are on much lower salaries, often working in legal aid.

A second way of undoing generalisations is to suggest a thought experiment. If someone says it always bad to lie, pose this scenario: 'If the mafia came to your front door during Sunday lunch and asked where your father was so they could shoot him, would you tell the truth and say he was at the dining room table or would you lie and say he was somewhere else?' Most people would decide to lie. Thought experiments are great ways to stress test a generalisation to see if it works. (So much so that, Philip Cam argues, counterexamples and thought experiments are critical thinking tools in and of themselves.)[35]

A solution to these lazy, unsophisticated generalisations is to apply our own original, but non-patented, James Bond rule … 'Never say never (and never say always)'.

When actor Sean Connery finished playing the role of James Bond in the late 1960s, he said he would never play the part again. In 1983 he was offered an enormous amount of money to play James Bond one more time, and he took it. Someone challenged him, saying, 'But you said you would never play James Bond again'. His famous reply was 'never say never again'. Indeed, the film's title became *Never Say Never Again*.

There are many less extreme words – known as 'qualifiers' – that you can use to blunt a bad generalisation. They include 'usually', 'often', 'predominantly', 'frequently', 'regularly', 'sometimes', 'occasionally', 'rarely', 'seldom', 'once in a blue moon' and 'when hell freezes over'. You can also use qualifiers such as 'a lot of', 'some' or 'a few'. Each of these words allows you to think about the problem more subtly and be more nuanced in your discussions. They will help you be careful with data, evidence and statistics. They protect you and give others the option to argue with you without having to directly refute you. For example:

- Most of the data suggests the next quarter will be in recession.
- Few of our clients are happy with the new automated system.
- Our distributors almost always get the fresh produce to the supermarket within four hours.

And to use our earlier examples: 'Some Australians are loud'; 'British people are often reserved'; 'Most Scandinavians like IKEA'; 'Most swans are white'. It is all calmer and a lot more reasonable.

Consider using qualifiers to tame the generalisations using our 'James Bond rule'. You will rarely go wrong.

TRY IT OUT

How could you tame these unjust generalisations?

- Meetings at my company are a waste of time.
- Victorians are racist.
- Students from Toffee High are stuck up.
- U2 write the best songs.
- People have stopped using our website to order gardening equipment.
- Greens voters need a dose of reality.
- National Party voters need more empathy with vulnerable people.
- Sharon in accounts can't add up.
- Summer days are hot.

Fake news

Fake news is another peril. It has a long and ignoble history. In ancient Rome, Octavian circulated Mark Antony's will, in which Antony said he wanted to be buried with Egyptian pharaohs. The will was fake. In the nineteenth century, a *New York Sun* report listed the creatures astronauts had found on the moon. Charlene told the class Darlene cheated on the Maths test. People have been disseminating rubbish for as long as there have been people and rubbish. However, the past decade has seen a disturbing increase in its reach, scope, toxicity and impact. Any commitment to thinking clearly requires us to be proactive in recognising and dismissing fake news, at least for ourselves, and especially because of its ubiquity in the public sphere. Hopefully this section will help you do that more effectively.

Fake news is news that is factually false. It can be a real story with false elements, or it can be totally made up. Occasionally it might be a mistake caused by sloppy journalism. Sometimes it is *mis*information or satire which has been mistakenly believed. Often it is *dis*information – false facts deliberately made up to mislead.

Fake news is not about opinions, judgements or evaluations. It is not about stretched perspectives on real facts. It is not negative news, or 'news and views I don't like hearing'. It is about 'facts' that are made up. Facts that are, in fact, fiction.

Fake news can be incredibly hard to spot because its creators, or AI, are skilled at making it look indistinguishable from real news. Also, most people now get their news from social media feeds instead of reputable news platforms, so it is much easier for fake news to spread. Worryingly, fake news can spread through these feeds significantly more quickly that real news does – probably because it is often more racy and readable than genuine news.

FactCheck.org,[36] Snopes.com[37] and UNESCO have guides to help spot fake news. They are not foolproof, but they are far better than merely surfing feeds.

So ...

Check the source. Is it a credible media source? Is the book published by a respected third party? Is the journal article peer reviewed? Is the website authoritative or funded by someone reputable (this can be hard to spot)? Does the 'source' even exist? Also, if you go to a website and find one hard-to-believe story among a series of sober articles about tax or legislation, it is more likely to be real. On the other hand, if the hard-to-believe story is nestled in among 10 other hard-to-believe stories, it is more likely to be made up. For example, single articles on *The National Report* might appear to be true. However, when you go to the site (where articles include 'Trump shoots world record 39 under par, 12 holes in one, during golf outing' and 'Solar panels drain the sun's energy, experts say'[38]) it is clear the articles are entirely fictional.

How striking is the material? If the scoop of the century – alien landings or a perpetual motion machine – has just landed in your inbox, why is it only being reported in a fringe website? Why hasn't the ABC or the BBC or Al Jazeera picked it up? Are these news powerhouses too slow – or part of the deep state conspiracy? Or is it just that the 'news' is not credible and made up? Check how extraordinary a claim is.

How old is the source? If you click back, you might find that white hot news story is actually a couple of years old and has just been recycled to get more clicks. Snopes writes about a 2015 news story that said Louisiana had made cash payments illegal. It turned out the fake story was more than three years old (and wrong) but had just been given a new lease of life.[39]

Is there an 'echo chamber'? The same wrong fact could be circulating around the internet, looking like different stories or sources. It is possible that the incredible story proliferating on the internet is actually all linked back to one dodgy source. Seeing it in 10 different places doesn't make it 10 times truer.

Read the whole article. The headline is often tantalising clickbait that you could half believe. Once you have read the whole article, though, its amateurishness or satire might come through.

Is the proof real? An article may well provide facts and lead you to a number of sources. But check these. Sometimes the sources don't exist. Sometimes the sources say something very different to what is being claimed.

Check the author. Do they have a background in the area? Are they connected with a reputable place, such as a university or a reliable media outlet? Or are they blogging in their basement? More extremely: does the author exist at all? Fake news sites will sometimes make up the name of the author; you can work this out through internet searches of the author or their photo (sometimes the same photo will be used by different sites for multiple people).

Check the style of the article. Are the facts presented professionally or soberly? Or are the ASTOUNDING claims CAPITALISED, with a lot of EXCLAMATION MARKS!! and *italics!!*? If the report reads more like the guy at the pub breathing beer fumes all over you, you have reason to consider it to be fake news.

Use a fact checker. There are many sites whose role is to debunk fake news. If you are worried about something, you can go to one of them and double check. They include: FactCheck.org, Snopes.com, *The Washington Post* Fact Checker and PolitiFact.com.

Be careful of AI generated images, videos or voices. People have become increasingly good at spotting easy picture fakes – heads photoshopped onto other people, entire people clumsily inserted into places they have never been, etc. Other photos are real but don't depict what they say they do. A photo of a politician slapping her hand on her forehead is unlikely to be a photo of her hitting herself in frustration as part of a story about one of her failings. However, both AI and humans have become exponentially better at creating fake images to the point where they are undetectable from the real thing. A fake photo of an explosion near the American Pentagon in 2023 was shared widely on social media and caused the stock market to dip. This makes our reliance on the source of the photos we see even more important. In turn, it pushes us back to reputable news sources. These can still be found regardless of whether your political leanings are to the left or the right.

The fake news spotter checklist above would prevent some people from entering the fever swamp where fakery is trafficked as true. But some of the more devastating fake news could easily slip through the net we have sewn together above. What is to be done?

Fake or false news needs to be handled with all the tools in this handbook, not just those in this section. A judicious balance of scepticism for unsupported claims and trust for reliable experts will go a long way. And maybe some hopes and prayers …

TRY IT OUT

Why might these be suspiciously like 'fake news'?

- Sydnymorningherarld.com.au
- a photo showing the Australian prime minister sharing a beer with Vladimir Putin in a swimming pool
- a headline that says, 'Boat FULL of ASYLUM SEEKERS lands in MELBOURNE!'

The Dunning-Kruger effect

Ignorance more frequently begets confidence than does knowledge.

Naturalist Charles Darwin, 1871[40]

This is a cautionary tale that might make you feel a little better about your abilities – or a little worse. It is actually a cognitive bias, but we have transported it from that chapter because it relates strongly to the perils and pitfalls of forming your own view and listening unreflectively to others about their views.

The Dunning-Kruger effect states that people who are incompetent at something generally think they are much better at it than they are, and people who are good at something generally think they are worse at it than they are. It is based on a study done by David Dunning and Justin Kruger in their depressingly titled article 'Unskilled and Unaware of It: How Difficulties in Recognizing One's Own Incompetence Lead to Inflated Self-Assessment'.

In this study, college students were asked to do activities in logic, grammar and personal humour. The people in the bottom quartile thought they had done better than they had. Indeed, students in the bottom 12th percentile predicted on average that they had performed in the 62nd percentile. As Dunning and Kruger wrote, 'When people are incompetent in the strategies they adopt to achieve success and satisfaction, they suffer a dual burden: not only do they reach erroneous conclusions and make unfortunate choices, but their incompetence robs them of the ability to realize it'.[41] It is when students are taught more (about grammar in their example) that they start to realise how limited their abilities are in an area. This might explain why the Automobile Association of America found that eight out of 10 men believed they were above average drivers when of course it is impossible for more than five out of 10 men to be above average drivers.[42]

This links closely to understanding public affairs issues. On one hand, the more people know about an issue the more they realise how little they know. The dark side of the Dunning-Kruger effect is that the less someone knows about an issue, the more likely they are to have a strong opinion about it. It is by learning more about the issue that they often work out that the issue is complicated and nuanced. If you reflect on the confidence people have about their views on economic policy, artificial intelligence or other cultures, it can sometimes be in inverse proportion to how much they know about it. This places a burden, unfortunately, on those who know about Dunning-Kruger, to research, consider and reflect on public affairs issues that concern us all.

People knew this long before Dunning and Kruger wrote their article. Charles Darwin wrote about it in 1871 (see above), and our society has old aphorisms like 'empty vessels make the loudest noise' and 'a little knowledge is a dangerous thing'.

Hopefully this will make you feel a little better when a relative starts lecturing you about an issue he or she once spent five minutes reading about. And hopefully it provides motivation to ingest as much critical thinking as you can at the same time as exposing yourself to the news and views of the day.

TRY IT OUT

Suggest a rating from zero (least reliable opinion) to 10 (most reliable opinion) for the following situations at a family gathering. Why have you given these ratings?

- Your uncle, a postman, has discovered how Einstein's theory of relativity is wrong.
- Your aunt, a nuclear scientist, believes nuclear power is a good way of creating energy for society.
- Your cousin, a shoe salesman, thinks he is the funniest guy at the wedding and is planning a stand-up comic career.
- Your second cousin, an English graduate, keeps correcting everyone's grammar when they speak.
- Your 17-year-old niece thinks she is in the top 20 per cent of drivers on the road.
- Your aunt-in-law, twice removed, immigrated to Australia last year and tells you how our political system is a corrupt mess compared with Belgium, where she came from.
- Your brother, the sommelier, tells you how good the wine is.

Occam's razor

This thinking tool can be used to assess different arguments and points of view. It should help you with the potential perils of your own arguments, or those of others.

For example, at work, you find people are a little less friendly than they were a month or two ago. People don't smile at you in the lifts as much. Managers walk past you. You ask people on Monday how their weekend was, and you get some vague, short answers. Perhaps the whole firm has decided to freeze you out. Clandestine meetings have plotted how to make you feel invisible, belittled and demeaned. They have set target dates on your resignation, and nothing can stop them.

Or they could just be busy.

It is easy to construct a complicated narrative in your head, then find lots of details to confirm it (see confirmation bias, page 135). But the truth is often more prosaic. In short, the simplest explanation is often the correct one.

This principle is simple and goes back as far as Aristotle and then a group of medieval philosophers. It was most famously coined by the monk William of Ockham who wrote 'plurality should not be posited without necessity'.[43] William of Ockham was a theologian who eventually wrote that the Pope was a heretic. As a result, William of Ockham had to flee from France to Germany. In his case, the bastards really were out to get him. The phrase was attributed to him, with an altered spelling of his name, because he used this principle so often in his writings. The idea of it being a 'razor' came much later – either because the principle is used to shave away multiplicities or because it cuts true theories away from ones that are too complicated and thus more likely to be false.

Occam's razor has a long history in science. If a theory is simple, it is more able to be proved or falsified, which is a good thing. So, if you have two theories that predict the same thing, it is usually better to go for the simpler one. Astronomer and scientist Carl Sagan developed a corollary of this in his book *Broca's Brain*: 'extraordinary claims require extraordinary evidence'.[44] He applied this when looking at claims of UFO sightings. When someone driving through the Arizona desert at night sees strange lights in the sky, is it better to conclude that intergalactic aliens have travelled across light years to hang out in scrubland, or that it is merely a plane, an optical illusion or a tired driver?

People use Occam's razor in medicine as well. Interns, unless they are in the Serengeti, are advised, 'When you hear hoofbeats, think horses, not zebras'.[45] Although doctors should be diligent and vigilant, they shouldn't rush to diagnose cancer every time someone comes in with a symptom.

We can also use Occam's razor to come up with a view in politics. Imagine an African country with decades of reasonably free elections. The opposition leader leads the prime minister in the opinion polls for a year, then goes on to win the election. Is the proper explanation that the voting machines were all pre-programmed by shadowy companies to spit out the wrong results, that the opposition party used gangs of street children to fill out and stuff millions of fake ballots, that the true ballots were burned in dumpster fires, that election officials who refused to go along with the fraud were taken out the back by the opposition and shot, and that civil servants illegally used zip-drives to reverse the results for the prime minister? Or did the opposition just get more votes? Occam's razor gives us a pretty good idea.

Occam's razor is not foolproof (people *do* get cancer; some scientific theories *are* complicated; we had aliens visit our house just last week). But it is a trusty tool you can use to avoid paranoia, overcomplication and conspiracies in the public sphere.

TRY IT OUT

What are likely and unlikely reasons for the following situations? How could Occam's razor help you decide?

- Your best friend fails to invite you on a trip to the beach one day.
- You have had a headache for three days running.
- US President John F. Kennedy was assassinated by his own FBI in arrangement with the mafia and elements of the CIA.
- You are travelling on the road between Sydney and Melbourne and have been driving for six hours solid when you see flashing and zig-zagging lights in the sky in front of you.
- The state government rezones most property within five kilometres of the CBD to build medium density houses. This increases the land value substantially. The state premier owns a house within five kilometres of the CBD.
- Your kitchen is messy.

Playing devil's advocate

When looking for a reasonably reliable 'truth' or reliably supported opinion, it's easy to get caught in an echo chamber that reinforces and strengthens your point of view. If you believe in lower rates of immigration, you will find plenty of evidence that more and more strongly supports your argument. If you believe in higher immigration, you will also find plenty of evidence that lends increasing weight to your view. But your argument won't have become much stronger – you will simply believe it more deeply. It's also easy to fall prey to rationalisation (assembling evidence to support your already firmly decided view) instead of reason (using evidence to decide your view).

A way to mitigate this is to play 'devil's advocate' – to search out and take seriously the other view (up to a point). This can be sometimes infuriating, but it's worth it.

The term 'devil's advocate' comes from the Latin 'advocatus diaboli'. It originated in the sixteenth century when the Vatican created a role, 'advocatus diaboli', to argue against the canonisation of potential saints. The advocatus diaboli was supposed to investigate whether the person up for sainthood had really performed miracles and whether, generally, they would be unsuitable. As the 'devil's advocate', they were against 'God's advocate' who would promote the person proposed for sainthood.

A great way to play devil's advocate is to regularly read material that offers a different world view to yours. If you are generally progressive, regularly read a respectable conservative news site. If you are generally conservative, regularly read a generally progressive news site. When you are reading articles you don't agree with, push on past the first few paragraphs.

Another way is to engage (respectfully) with people who have a very different view to you or are willing to engage with the opposite view. It will often be more interesting than talking about real estate prices or childcare. Use the 'one mouth, two ears' adage to help you learn more than you can teach. But be careful. Others might be less willing to play devil's advocate than you. It can be worthwhile to tell other people you are playing devil's advocate before you do it.

A third way is to play devil's advocate in your own head. Simply pull yourself up by asking yourself what the other argument would be. If you are in favour of higher immigration, push yourself into lower immigration arguments, and vice versa. This connects to the adage 'never judge a person until you have walked a mile in their shoes'. Ask what you would think about the issue if you were a police officer or a refugee or a financier or any number of other individuals.

A more sophisticated version of this can be found in philosopher John Rawls' 'Mind Game'.[46] Rawls asked people to imagine they were about to enter a new society with one catch: they didn't know who they would be when they got there. He calls this the 'veil of ignorance'. They could be rich, poor, male, female, the elite or the marginalised. They didn't know what traits they would have – they could be smart or the opposite. They could be sporty or club-footed. They could look like a god or Quasimodo. With no knowledge of who they would be, they were then asked to make the laws and rules of the society. The idea is that, stripped of all self -interest, the laws of the society would be the fairest possible.

Let's apply this to the issue of how much power the police should have. You don't know whether you are going to be a police officer, a person whose family has a bad history with police officers, a victim of a crime, the wealthiest person in society, a poor and hungry person, someone untouched by crime or someone accused of a crime. Without this knowledge, decide what powers the police should have in a civil society. You might be surprised where you land.

Playing devil's advocate is only effective up to a point. If you do not believe the country is in the grip of Satanic arsonists, you don't have to spend a lot of time reading sites that say it is. This would create a false equivalence. There are not two substantial sides to every story. Climate science and climate denialism don't deserve equal time. Neither does liberal democracy versus Nazism, or 'Charles Manson was mean' versus 'Charles Manson was misunderstood'. You don't need to give the drunk bigot on one side of you at a wedding equal time with the professor of politics or state premier who is sitting on the other (unless the drunk bigot is also your betrothed).

But in a world increasingly gripped in partisan gridlock, with people stuck inside their own echo chambers, halls of mirrors or bell jars, playing devil's advocate can be an important civic tonic.

TRY IT OUT

Articulate your opinions on the things below for 10 seconds, then spend a minute or two on each one to come up with your best version of the opposite opinion (not the one that's easiest to knock, but the best version):

- your suburb
- eating meat grown in a lab
- abortion
- whether we should align more closely strategically and economically with Europe or Asia
- public schools and independent schools
- travelling by air
- stretching yourself financially to buy a house
- the representation of Indigenous people in parliaments
- the top tax rate, and whether it should be higher or lower
- vegetarianism.

Has your original view been disrupted or shaken?

STATISTICS – PERILS AND PITFALLS

There are three kinds of lies: lies, damned lies, and statistics.

Author Mark Twain[47]
('quoting' Benjamin Disraeli, who did not say it)

Your son comes home and reports he got 65 per cent in his English test.

'That's okay, I guess,' you say.

'But the average mark in the class was eighty-five per cent,' he says.

'That's not great then,' you say.

'And I came last,' he says.

'That's a problem then,' you say.

'But most people in my class were away – only five people did it, and that includes the dux,' he says.

'Oh ... well, that puts a different spin on it,' you say.

'And sixty-five per cent was the top mark in the class next door that did the same test – and there's twenty in that class,' he says.

'That's great,' you say, thinking your son would have topped the class next door.

'But there are ten classes, and the average mark was seventy per cent,' he says.

'That's still okay, I guess,' you say.

'But the *median* mark across the ten classes is eighty-five per cent, not seventy per cent,' he says.

'Well, er, that's not too good then,' you mumble.

'But across the last decade, kids who have done this same test have averaged sixty per cent, so I'm above average for that,' he says.

'Um, well, er, maybe that's sort of good then,' you say.

'But across the state, the average for that test is eighty per cent,' he says and takes a breath.

'Please go to another room,' you say.

In a similar but less torturous vein, psychologist Diane Halpern provides the example of turning pure fat into a 96 per cent fat-free product.[48] 'Take two pats of butter, which are 100 per cent fat. You could eat them. Or you could drop them into a large glass of water and drink the whole revolting concoction. You have just consumed a 96 per cent fat-free drink.'

Numbers can be clarifying, neutralising weak assertions with a few hard-hitting facts. But they can also confuse and mislead, depending on how they are used. They can open a vista or show you just one tiny part of the landscape. The more you are armed with a few techniques to handle and use them, the better.

Watch the denominator: You hear that 15 arts projects were funded by the state government last year, so you think you will put in an application. There are many factors that might mean you succeed or fail – how good your project is, how talented you are, etc. But probably the biggest factor is how many applications there are in total (ie the denominator). If 30 people put in applications this year, you've got a pretty good chance (15/30 – a half-half chance). If 3000 people put in applications, your chances are much, much smaller (15/3000 = a half of one per cent chance, all other things being equal). Only 1 in 200 applications will succeed, so no matter how good your arts project is, you are probably going to struggle. And much of your prospect of succeeding comes down to the denominator.

Watch out for the denominator when considering health statistics too. For example, you hear that five people die in your state each day from the new disease slothpox. Before you start panicking or relaxing, work out how many people are in your state. If it is an overcrowded urban jungle with 60 million people, your chance of dying each day is .0000083 per cent. If your state is a sparsely populated wasteland populated by tumbleweeds and just 500 people, your chance of dying is one per cent per day – time to pack up the car. Other factors matter, of course – it is very different if it has been five people a day for a year, or if it was one person two days ago and 20 people yesterday and 100 people today. But the denominator matters.

Linked to this is the issue of sample size. You read an article that says, '30 per cent of people report to researchers they used cocaine in the past year'. But how many people did the researchers ask? Was it 20 – which is pretty unreliable – or was it 50,000 which makes it much more reliable? Again, other questions come into play, such as whether people were asked at a retirement village or outside a meth lab or somewhere else. However, the sample size is significant.

Watch the mean (ie the average): Imagine a country with an average salary of $200,000. That doesn't sound too bad at first – a utopia of high living standards. But just because the average salary is $200,000, don't presume anyone actually gets this amount. It could be that every person is earning $200,000 a year. Or it could be that one in 10 people earn just under $2,000,000 a year and the other nine earn $10,000 a year. This place would be hugely unequal, with most of the population struggling and in poverty. But the mean salary – $200,000 – is the same. When you hear about a mean salary or mark, be sure to also ask about the spread of actual numbers – are they clustered around the mean or is there a gigantic difference?

Watch the difference between the mean and the median: You might be getting hot and sweaty just thinking about the difference here. Often, 'median' and 'mean' are used interchangeably to convey some version of 'the average'. But they are very different.

Imagine you have just completed your university examinations and for five different subjects you got 100, 95, 95, 55 and 0 marks (you hated the subject you got 55 for, and your alarm didn't go off so you missed the last exam completely). You need a good story for your parents, who are paying your university fees.

Your mean mark is these five marks added up and then divided by the number of exams you did: 100+95+95+55+0 divided by 5 = 69 per cent. But 69 per cent doesn't sound great.

You could look at your median mark – the middle one. You got five marks, so the middle one is the third one: 100, 95, **95**, 55, 0 – 95 per cent! Much better. Your median mark will mean a happy home reunion … unless of course your parents know something about statistics and ask for the mean (or all your exam marks).

Regression to the mean. Your favourite football player has just had the game of his career, scoring half-a-dozen goals and dominating the opposition. Great, you think. You will go and watch him at his next game and cheer him on as he slays the hapless opposition again. But he has a pretty good, not great, game. He is in a lot of play and scores a goal – but nothing like his career high of the week before. What has happened? Has he started going downhill already, his glory days behind him? Or is he just snapping back to the way he most often plays?

We tend towards thinking that if something is extreme once, it will keep being extreme in the future (the best episode of your favourite television series, the best century scored by a cricketer, etc). However, it is generally more likely to revert to something closer to the average. In other words, it will 'regress to the mean'. In sport it is sometimes known as the '*Sports Illustrated* jinx', because once you appear on the cover of *Sports Illustrated*, your next few games are likely to be worse.

Moving off the sports field, imagine you matchmake the best-looking guy you know with the best-looking girl you know. They marry and have children – the best-looking kids the world has ever seen, right? Again, wrong. The kids are more likely to be less good looking than either their mum or their dad. Extreme characteristics in parenthood are less likely to be passed on to their children. The children regress closer to the average.

Even in a class where there are 10 assignments, different students are likely to have good days and bad days. Different people will top different tests and different people will come bottom. By the end of the year the class marks will be a little closer to average.

The same goes for your trading performance or launching your first startup. You might be the next big thing. But it is not a crushing defeat if instead you regress to your own mean.

Regression to the mean can also help explain many miracle cures. For example, you are sick with a cold. Someone tells you that a horseradish, garlic and soil concoction works wonders. You try it, keep it down, and within a few days your cold has disappeared. 'It works,' you think. Possibly. But it's more likely you just got better naturally – your body has regressed to the mean of being healthy. After all, most head colds fix themselves in a couple of days. But instead of attributing it to reverting to the health mean, you credit the miracle (yet suspect) cure. Many vitamin and herbal remedies industries rely on this reversion to the mean (and a heavy dose of unfalsifiability as well).

When you see an unusually high or extreme number (skyrocketing house prices, high football scores, a company's profit margin, a popular politician's polls) don't assume it's the beginning of a trend or that it is going to stay this good/bad. Consider instead that these numbers are more likely to track back to average, or to average levels of growth. Of course, that's not always the case – property has frequently stayed up, and shares in some companies just keep rising and rising. But this is a long way from being the rule. It might help save your ego, your long-term confidence and your bank balance if you are thinking of buying or investing.

Fake precision: Using fake or detailed numbers can make someone sound more authoritative. If we told you using this book had been shown to make you twice as good at formulating clear arguments, you might think that was pretty good – in a rubbery sort of way. But if we said, 'Using this book is shown to make you 63 per cent better at formulating clear arguments', you might be quite impressed by both the number and the lifestyle opportunity it provides. Yet the precision of 63 per cent is absurd. It is impossible to measure 'ability to argue' with this level of exactitude.

Precise statistics are everywhere, from the proportion of people who lose weight on a diet to the percentage of medium-size businesses that prosper five years after startup. Don't trust them (at least 87 per cent of the time!).

Diane Halpern provides a good example from Mark Twain, that statistical wag from the start of the chapter. Twain once said the Mississippi River was 100,000,003 years old. When asked how he could be so precise, he replied he was told the river was 100 million years old three years earlier.[49]

Extrapolating: This is a mathematical trend that can lead to some very strange results. It takes a trend in numbers and assumes that trend will keep going in the future at about the same rate.[50] For example, the average woman in 1960 had five children. Now it is 2.5. It has fallen steadily every year in between. If we continue that trend line, in 2080 women will be having no children at all. You can't keep extrapolating a trend line, particularly when the phenomenon has a ceiling or a floor.

Statistics on graphs: Statistics presented graphically are often easy to digest. But don't be fooled. When statistics are in graphs, you have to worry about the statistic *and* the graph.[51]

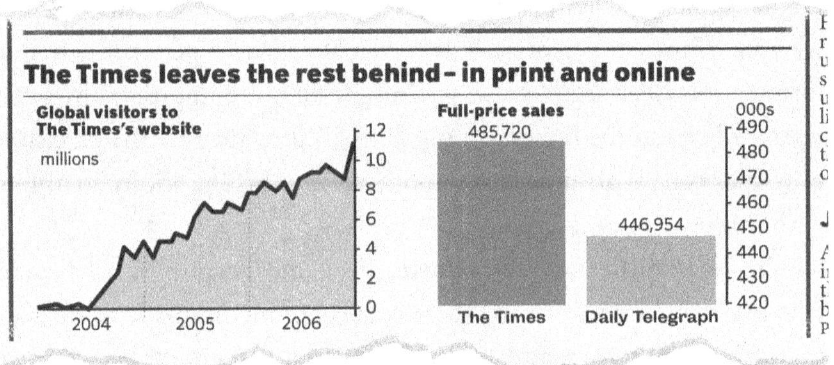

52

Firstly, graphs can mislead you by not starting the columns at zero. A quick look at the graph here makes it looks like the *Times* is selling twice as many copies as the *Daily Telegraph*, when it is only actually about 10 per cent more (485,720 against 446,954). The problem with the graph is that it starts at 420, not zero. A graph that started the y axis at 0 would be much less impressive.

Here's another that shows what looks like an alarming rise in the rate of welfare – has it really tripled in just two years?

Well, a closer look at the vertical axis paints a very different picture. The number of people getting welfare has actually gone from 97 million to 106 million. Still a noticeable rise, but more like 10 per cent than 200 per cent.

THE BLOG

Over 100 million Now Receiving Federal Welfare

2.40PM, AUG 8 2012 • BY DANIEL HALPER

A new chart set to be released later today by the Republican side of the Senate Budget Committee details a startling statistic: "Over 100 Million People in the U.S. Now Receiving Some Form Of Federal Welfare."

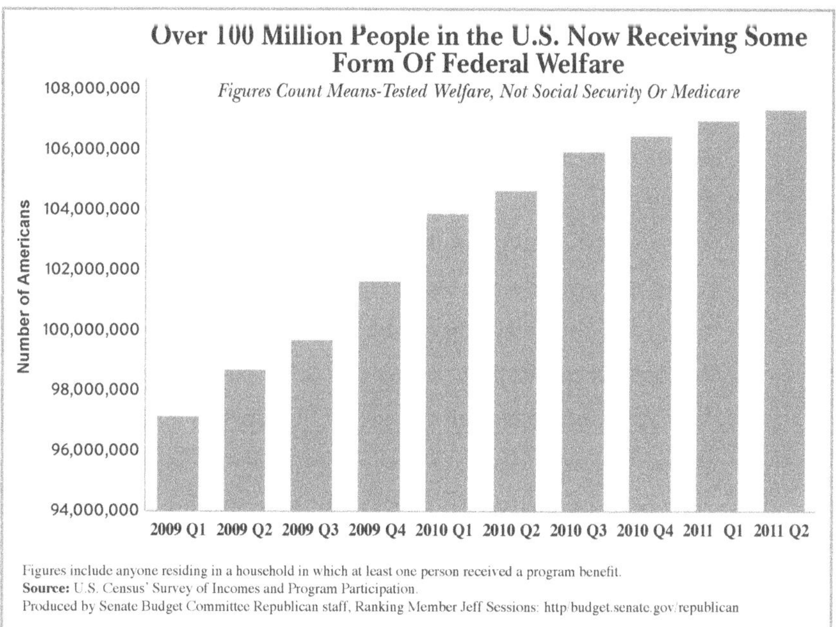

53

TRY IT OUT

Each of the following statistics is questionable. What additional statistical questions should be asked? (Hint: these questions are in the same order as the techniques explained above.)

- Enrico comes second in a local painting contest. You don't know whether this is a big deal or not.
- In Maria's home town, the annual rate of death from cancer has doubled in the past 12 months. It is also five times what it was in the 10 years previous. Should she move out?
- You are about to get a job at the tech firm Disrupticon. They tell you the average salary is $300,000, and you are going for an average job. What should you watch out for before mentally banking the $300,000 each year?
- You are the top trader out of 100 traders in your firm in June. You were also the top trader in May. Before that, you were in the top 10 traders, but never number one. Should you look forward to being the top trader in the firm in August and September?
- You're told a new face cream reduces spots and wrinkles by 47 per cent.
- Your amazing new startup has grown by 1000 per cent in the first year! You started it alone and now you have 10 employees.
- Bonus question: if we extrapolated this in a linear way, how many years is it before you are employing the whole population of Earth?

(Hint: it's less than 15 years.)

CHAPTER 3
BUILDING MORE SKILFUL ARGUMENTS

In this chapter we will dive into the components that make up an argument and the different types of reasoning. You won't be spouting these in a management meeting or university tutorial any time soon, but what comes next will hopefully lodge in the back of your mind and make your thinking clearer, more structured and more explicit.

We're told about the different parts of our bodies – our legs, our arms, our fingers, our toes – from our very earliest days. But what about our reasoning? We use our brain as much as our body, but we're usually totally unpractised at naming the different parts of our rational thinking. Let's change that.

The *Oxford English Dictionary* defines argument as 'an assertion or fact put forward in order to persuade or sway others; a reason advanced in support of (or in opposition to) a proposition.' It comes from the classical Latin, *argumentum*, meaning 'process of reasoning'. This was associated with proof, particularly mathematical.

Arguments are a key part of reasoning. An argument isn't just two people at a bar having a verbal punch-up. An argument is a belief or claim that is also connected with a reason for that belief.

If you do a mental audit, you'll find you are making arguments all the time, even if it's just 'The price of petrol is low, I had better fill up', or 'Judy just blanked me – I think I offended her' or 'There's that liar and cheat on TV again, no way am I voting for her'.

Let's look at a particular argument (a belief supported by a reason): Judy just blanked me – I think I offended her. There's a belief/opinion in there – that you have offended Judy. And there is a reason for this belief – she just blanked you.

Of course, the argument might not all be true. Judy might not have blanked you at all; she might just be having a bad day, or you might be paranoid. You might or might not have offended her. Nonetheless, the structure of the statement is still an argument.

Sometimes a list of statements can masquerade as an argument without actually being one; for example, 'Kids are spending longer on Instagram. They are spending longer on Snapchat. They are spending longer on TikTok. They spend up to seven hours a day on social media.' You can feel the other part of the argument in there; it is probably something like 'Kids spend too long on social media' (although it could also be 'How lucky kids are today to have these wonderful tools at their disposal'). But there is no belief stated explicitly, so it is not an argument.

A collection of beliefs or opinions can also look deceptively like an argument without actually being one:[54] 'Cocaine should be illegal, any idiot knows that'. 'Any idiot' is just there for emphasis. It is not a reason. And an argument must have a reason. The statement is an opinion but not an argument.

Although there is a panoply of books that explain arguments, *Critical Thinking* by Brooke Moore and Richard Parker is particularly clear. They are professors from the University of California and their book is now in its fourteenth edition. We have relied on it, among others, and can recommend it.

CLAIMS

A claim is the most basic building block of critical thinking – and of most conversations you have day to day. It is a statement[55] that expresses an opinion or belief.[56]

Claims can be proven or unproven, true or false. A claim can be a premise or a conclusion.

Many claims are unremarkable: 'The door is closed'; 'The newsagent is open'; 'Insects have six legs'; 'The sky is blue'. No one is going to argue with you for suggesting them.

Other claims require more thinking, evidence, evaluation and care: 'We should close all coal mines by the end of the decade'; 'I am going to marry my girlfriend'; 'My boss is out to get me'; 'People who go to pubs are argumentative thugs'.

Some claims are wild and woolly and go even further. They are still claims: 'Capitalism is out to get me'; 'We are living in a virtual reality simulation'; 'The world is run by little green goblins no one can see'. These claims are problematic because they are just about impossible to prove or disprove.[57]

PREMISES AND CONCLUSIONS

Premises and conclusions are subsets of claims.

Premise: Chris picked up his umbrella before he went out the door.

Conclusion: It is raining outside.

A premise is a proposition or a reason for believing a conclusion.[58] A conclusion is the point of view or statement that you are trying to establish – the purpose of the argument.[59]

In many arguments the premise comes first. Sometimes you'll want to start with the conclusion and then build in the premise or support afterwards: 'It is raining outside, because I just saw Chris pick up his umbrella before he went out the door'.

The conclusion about the rain is a pretty good one, but not watertight. It is probably raining. But it might be just cloudy now and Chris is cautious. Chris might use the umbrella as a walking stick. Chris might be a Russian spy off to poison someone with the lethal hypodermic syringe in the tip of his umbrella.

Premises and conclusions are also the bedrocks of issue-based arguments. For example, you might want to argue against the death penalty using the following premises and conclusions:

> **Premise 1:** South Nankrumpet has the death penalty for murder and the murder rate is the same as other states.
>
> **Premise 2:** North Nankrumpet has the death penalty for traffic offences and its traffic offences are the same as other states.
>
> **Conclusion:** The death penalty does not act as a deterrent against crimes.

This conclusion – 'the death penalty does not act as a deterrent against crimes' – can be made because of the premises. Without the premises, your conclusion about the death penalty is just an assertion.

These premises don't make the conclusion watertight, but they are much better than nothing. Nonetheless, there are a few cautions we must make about premises.

Firstly, as Brooke Moore and Richard Parker point out, a premise can only properly support the conclusion if it is true.[60] If you have incorrect premise information about the traffic infringement rates in North Nankrumpet, your conclusion looks shaky.

Secondly, other premises/reasons might change or modify your conclusion. Perhaps North Nankrumpet's traffic offences were five times as bad as other states before the death penalty was introduced and now their traffic offences are just the same as other states. Perhaps 50 per cent of North Nankumptians, as they are led to their place of execution, lament, 'If only I had realised that driving over the speed limit would result in my death, I wouldn't have done it'.

Thirdly, a premise can also only support a conclusion if it is relevant to the conclusion. You could tell someone about the levels of education, healthcare, peace, harmony, civil accord and birdwatching in North Nankrumpet, but these premises won't tell you much about whether the death penalty reduces crime rates there.

Even with all these cautions, though, the conclusion about the death penalty is stronger because premises support it.

If you want to make it clear you are using premises/reasons in your discussions or reports, you can use signposts such as 'given that', 'in the first place', 'as indicated by' or even 'because'. If you want to make it clear you are stating a conclusion, you could say 'consequently', 'therefore' or 'so'.

When you are making arguments or assessing other people's arguments, you rarely say 'my premises are'. But if you can identify the premises and conclusions in your head, they can form a hidden structure that will make your arguments stronger and more convincing.

DEFINITIONS

A definition is a statement that takes a word or expression and explains what it means. Definitions are the white chalk that mark out the field of your game, debate or argument.

People should agree on definitions so that they at least agree on what they are arguing about. A definition should not become the argument itself. For example, a 'progressive' can be defined as 'a woke, humourless person who wants to take money earned by people who deserve it and give it to people who didn't earn it and don't deserve it'. A conservative can be defined as 'a backwards-looking bigot who either doesn't notice or doesn't care about their own unfair privilege'.

Any discussion about conservatism or progressiveness is going to get nowhere with these 'definitions' because the person's actual argument has been shipped into the definition. The definition has become the game itself instead of the field marker of the game. Be on the lookout to make sure your definitions are as neutral as possible ... and make sure other people aren't hoodwinking you with dodgy definitions.

Moore and Parker[61] point out three types of definitions. Let's try them out ... on a dog.

The most common is the **analytical definition**, which points out the features something must have. For example, a dog, according to the *Oxford English Dictionary*, is 'a domesticated carnivorous mammal ... which typically has a long snout, an acute sense of smell, non-retractile claws and a barking, howling or whining voice'. That will help in telling the difference between a dog and a cat or a cow or a chair.

The second type of definition is one **by example**: 'Lulu next door is a dog, and Patches down the street is a dog, but Aunt Mabel's Marmaduke is not a dog because it is a lion'.

The third is **by synonym**, where you just replace the word being defined with another word or phrase that means the same thing. A dog can be defined as 'pooch', 'canine' or 'hound'.

So how do you spot or use a good definition? Firstly, it should be clear. Don't use complicated words that end up making the concept even more confusing. Secondly, it should be something people generally agree on and should not tip the scale to help one side of the argument or the other (see the point about 'progressives' and 'conservatives'). And finally, it should also be open enough to allow for ambiguity for big issues. For example, if you define 'freedom' or 'human rights' or 'mind' for a debate with completeness and agreement, you might find you have already solved the problem and achieved something that thousands of years of philosophy have not.

ISSUES

An 'issue' is the heart of what the claims in an argument might be about. It is a way of working out the matter that the argument concerns before taking a side. The claim 'workers need a higher minimum wage' leads upstream to the issue 'wage levels for workers'. Identifying the issue early can make your eventual arguments sound more reasoned and well thought out.

Working out the issue before you present your argument can lead you to all sorts of investigations to get opinions, evidence, statistics, economic theories, etc. This will improve your ultimate argument. Looking at it the other way around, making an argument is a good way of thinking through issues. Either way they are closely connected.

EVIDENCE (AGAIN)

We have already written about evidence in chapter 2, but it is also worthwhile to think of it as part of the anatomy of an argument. Philosopher Robert Arp defines it nicely in his book *Bad Arguments*: '[Evidence is] a fact or concept … that provides support (affirmation, confirmation, corroboration, proof substantiation, verification) for the truth or falsity of a claim'.[62] In an argument, evidence would generally be a premise in support of your conclusion.

If a claim is unremarkable (for example, Scotland is north of England) you don't need to buy a bus ticket to the English/Scottish border to check for yourself. You don't really need much evidence for generally accepted claims. More remarkable claims require more evidence. If your friend told you aliens had landed on the English/Scottish border, you would want some pretty stiff proof.

A great deal of complex evidence is needed if you want to make a more complex statement or a value judgement, such as 'reducing company tax helps people on the lowest wages' or 'private healthcare is no good for the country'. Many people will expect a lot of substantiation for such a big conclusion. You also need to look for a weight or preponderance of evidence. Someone can cherrypick evidence for almost anything, but it won't make their conclusions much stronger. You must weigh the evidence and work out which is more convincing.

It seems unremarkable to say claims require evidence. However, society has shown that merely making assertions over and over again can have the same effect on people as providing evidence. This implies that if you don't have any evidence, fine – just make the claim or assertion again, but louder.

COUNTERARGUMENTS

These are arguments that refute your conclusion.[63] It is often good to bake them into your argument to show that you have considered them but haven't been persuaded by them. Most arguments have two sides and someone else will probably bring up the other side, so you might as well get there first.

For example, you might say, 'Our Scrabble distribution outlet should open a new store in the next city for reasons w, x and y. It is possible we might over-extend ourselves and our debt might get too high, but we can derisk this by doing a, b and c, and on balance it is still a good idea because k, j and l.' For anticipating the counterarguments your boss will give you double points.

QUALIFIERS

Sometimes you will need or want to put a restriction on your conclusion. You can do this with a qualifier. This can make your argument much safer, particularly if you are pitching something. As Diane Halpern states in her excellent book *Thought and Knowledge*, 'a qualifier states the conditions under which the conclusion is valid. It sets limits or constraints on the conclusion.'[64]

You might say, 'If I finish this assignment, I think I will go out for dinner tonight, unless it pours rain.' You are qualifying your conclusion. On a less domestic front, a government official could say, 'I think this tax cut is a good idea, and we can finance it with increased economic activity, as long as we do not tip into a recession in the next year'. The official has just made the case more careful and given themself some future wriggle room.

INFERENCES

An inference is a tentative conclusion formed from known facts.[65] An example is: 'I think I cooked my new curry poorly because my partner stopped eating it after two bites'. A key feature of an inference is the admission that you are not quite sure but you think you have some decent evidence. In the case of the curry, it could indeed be that you put too much spice in, that it is too hot, or that the meat is undercooked. There are all sorts of ways in which you could have cooked it badly. On the other hand, it could be that your partner ate on the way home. It might be the best curry in the world, but your partner was angling for pizza and is upset that you didn't pick up the signs. Or perhaps your partner was sacked a few hours earlier, is looking for a way to tell you and just isn't interested in food. There are all sorts of ways in which your inference that you cooked your curry poorly might or might not be true. But it's good to at least make an inference – if your partner doesn't eat their food, it would generally be better to think about why.

We make inferences all the time. The world fills us with data of all kinds, and we don't have time to Sherlock Holmes our way through every minute of every day and interrogate each piece to a 98 per cent chance of truth. So, we make reasonable inferences. At the same time, we have to make sure our inferences don't become 100 per cent proof in our heads. This would be jumping to a conclusion. If the inference that you made a rubbish curry became proof to you, then you might stop making curry when you are actually a fantastic curry chef.

ASSUMPTIONS

Assumptions are statements made without proof. They are similar to inferences but stronger. Sometimes they are correct: 'You are coming at me with a knife, so I assume you are pretty upset about something' is a pretty reasonable assumption unless you work in a sushi restaurant. But often they lead to sloppy arguments full of holes.

Assumptions are often hidden or subconscious. As a result, they can be harder to spot than inferences. This is okay if the assumption is trivial or obvious. Consider: 'They were in the dining room when the lights blacked out and they were plunged into darkness'. The assumption is that the blackout happened at night-time. This is trivial. On the other hand, the assumption is not okay if it is controversial or wrong. For example, the statement 'Going nude in public doesn't hurt anyone, so everyone should be able to do it' makes the controversial assumption that people should be able to do anything in public that doesn't hurt other people. This assumption is obvious when it's pointed out but could quietly slip by otherwise.

Assumptions are also beliefs that you might not want to examine too closely in order to keep your life simpler. They might be assumptions such as 'I assume politicians are crooks' or 'I assume everyone in my church is a moral person'. They often don't stand up to interrogation.

There are frequently hidden assumptions in advertising. For example, the advertising line 'Twice as many people use Sparklz toothpaste than any other toothpaste' assumes that popularity is a sign of quality, and that Sparklz is a better toothpaste to buy.[66] Advertisers can be excellent at stashing assumptions into arguments, so we should be equally excellent at pulling them out again.

EXPLANATIONS

An explanation is a type of premise. Except that instead of being a 'reason' it will be a 'cause'; for example, 'The water in the kettle boiled because we plugged the kettle in and turned it on'.

This is just cause and effect. It's hard to have much of a disagreement about plugging in a kettle as a reason for it boiling (unless you are in the middle of a blackout, in which case it is just spooky).

In practice, reasons and explanations can look quite similar.[67] Take this example: 'I am late for my lecture because I missed the train'. This is the cause of you being late for the lecture, and thus it is an explanation. But is it enough of a reason for an argument? Perhaps 'I am late for my lecture because I slept in and missed the train' would be better. Even better might be 'I am late for my lecture because I am a disorganised slob who never cares about what time I get up to catch the train'. Now *that* is a reason.

IS MY ARGUMENT ANY GOOD: THE HALPERN METHOD

In *Thought and Knowledge*, Diane Halpern offers a three-step method to check the quality of an argument. Run this 'Halpern method' through a presentation, a paper or the lecture you are about to give your aged parents. An argument that passes all three steps is also known as a 'sound' argument.

Are your premises acceptable and consistent?[68] For the premise to be acceptable, it basically must be true. An earlier chapter wades into the murky waters of truth (see page 42), but here's a quick refresher.

Something you say could be true for several different reasons. Firstly, it could be true because it is unremarkable common knowledge: 'The suburb of Truman is 10 miles south of the city centre'. It could also be true because you have personal experience of it: 'It usually takes me 30 minutes to get from my home in Truman to work in peak hour'. Often you can accept something as true because many people, including experts, agree on it, even though we don't have any first-hand knowledge of it: 'Proxima Centauri is the closest star to earth'.

Premises in an argument can often be wrong, and this makes the whole argument shaky. 'It takes me an hour to get to work' (it might feel like an hour but it's only half an hour). 'There is a rich seam of oil under this field' (you should have checked that more thoroughly before you started commercial drilling). As you can imagine, 'check your premises aren't wrong' takes a moment to write and a lifetime to master.

Your premises also need to be consistent with each other. If you are trying to argue the conclusion that you should be able to invade a neighbouring country, it would be inconsistent to say, 'In the past the country next door was accepted by the West as a part of our country' and 'The imperialist West today doesn't get to tell us where our borders are'. Either you rely upon international opinion or you don't.

Do the premises support the conclusion? Not all premises are equal in bolstering a conclusion.

Any issue will generally have a number of true premises. Not all will be useful. Some will be almost completely irrelevant. Don't use these at all. Some will be helpful, but a bit weak: you might need a lot of them to support a conclusion.[69] But sometimes one or two premises are so relevant and convincing that they support the conclusion all on their own. You'll only need one or two of these.

Perhaps you are considering taking the train to your city job from your home in Truman and selling your second car. The premise 'There is great coffee just outside the train station right next to my work' is irrelevant. It is true: it is the best coffee in town. But you can get that coffee regardless of whether you take the train or not, because the café is right next to your work. A weak premise might be 'Simone in accounting takes the train and likes it'. That's okay, but Simone only lives two stations away, so it's much quicker for her. Another weak premise might be: 'I'll get money for selling the car'. True, but weak – your car is a bomb, and you won't get much money for it. A strong supportive premise could be 'A new metro station just opened a block from our house' or 'The traffic has become so much worse, it's gridlock every day'. These statements, presuming they are also true, are strong reasons. They could hold up the argument to take public transport all on their own.

When looking at your premises in an argument, don't settle for them merely being true. Rather, assess how much they actually support the argument you want to make. This will also help you work out how much weight you want to give them.

Is something missing? This is often the most overlooked part in putting together a brilliant argument … and it's often the part that will sink it. You have put together a fantastic dossier about why a coffee shop would be great in this suburb but overlooked the fact that there are 'no stopping' signs for half a kilometre on both sides of the road. You decided to go to Nepal during your mid-year break because of the beautiful, rugged mountain scenery, but overlooked the fact that it was monsoon season. You were convinced by a politician who advocated a big increase in the tax rate to fund education and health, but who omitted figures about its impact on economic activity. You became annoyed when someone got ahead of you on an affirmative action program but ignored generations of ingrained disadvantage.

'Is something missing?' is a difficult one to guard yourself against. It is one thing to judge a statement right in front of you, but another to go looking for what's not even there now (and possibly ever!). This is why missing but important factors can sting you by surprise later.

One way of dealing with this is to play 'devil's advocate' (see page 81). Try arguing the opposite point of view and see what comes up. Research the opposite point of view too. In the case of more personal arguments, step into the other person's shoes and see it from their point of view or with their background. Another way is to simply ask yourself and others the question 'What are we missing?' It is an uncomfortable question that people in a meeting often just try to wait out, but rescanning the landscape can sometimes come up with a previously unconsidered factor.

SECTION II
CHALLENGES TO SOUND THINKING

CHAPTER 4
COGNITIVE BIASES

FAST AND SLOW THINKING

Psychologist and Nobel laureate Daniel Kahneman (1934–2024) has opened up a whole new area of analysing how we think and how we act. He has shown that what we believe are our clever, reasoned, conscious choices are often powered deep down by weird, unconscious drivers. He has been instrumental in identifying, testing, collecting and writing about dozens of biases humans have almost always without knowing it. And he doesn't mean biases like 'I hate that chicken shop up the road' or 'I am biased against vegetarians', but deep-seated, cognitive, architecture-of-the-brain biases. He worked very closely with his colleague, psychologist Amos Tversky, who also published extensively in the area before his premature death in 1996.

Reading about this can be both frightening and exciting: frightening because you reflect on how many of your decisions were (and still will be) powered by parts of your mind that you can barely control; exciting because at least if you know about these biases, you can get in the way of many of them, think much more clearly and make better decisions as a result. Awareness of 'sunk cost fallacy', 'confirmation bias' or 'planning fallacy' could change your life. Put together all 14 of the biases listed here and they probably will.

Kahneman's masterwork is *Thinking, Fast and Slow* (2011).[70] It has inspired dozens of books and chapters – including this one. The beginning of Kahneman's work on biases is what he calls 'System 1' and 'System 2' thinking (although these terms were used before him). Basically, 'System 1' thinking is our fast instincts, and 'System 2' thinking involves our slow and deliberate thought.

When we were hunter-gatherers, we were hardly at the top of the food chain. Lions, tigers and bears could eat us. Even a sufficiently agitated giraffe could and would kill us. We relied on subtle signs from the environment – a rustle in the grass, an unexpected noise, something in the corner of our eye – to alert us to danger. The better we got at this, the more likely we were to survive. This thinking was fast – basically instinctive, System 1 thinking. We didn't have time to contemplate whether the rustle in the grass was a lion, a figment of our imagination or a more statistically likely wind pocket. By then we could have been lunch. Instead, we just got out of there. System 1 thinking regularly saved our lives.

System 2 thinking is different. It is slow. It is the careful, reasonable combining of information. It is using logic, reason, data, statistics and experience to come up with a conclusion. Basically, it is the rest of this chapter. When deciding which of two job offers to take, we will usually use System 2 thinking. We'll weigh up evidence, compare the job descriptions, read the companies' material and research their reputations. None of this would have been of much use 200,000 years ago, but for many of the complex issues that face us in the modern world, System 2 thinking is the way to go.

But our brain and our body love that fast System 1. They are used to using it – it's been saving our lives for hundreds of thousands of years, and it still does in emergencies. When you do things 'on a whim', when you 'go with your gut', when you 'just take a punt', you are using System 1 thinking. The brain is a muscle, and although it only takes up two per cent of our bodyweight, it uses 20 per cent of our energy.[71] If your body can get your thinking to take a shortcut, fantastic. It means less energy expended.

As a result, you can find yourself using System 1 thinking when you should use System 2. You jump to conclusions. You let cognitive biases rule. Some of them are so ingrained that it is almost impossible to overcome them; they are pre-installed in your system. Others can be worked on, though.

Let's do an example. Answer the following the question in less than one second:

> A bat and a ball together cost $11.
> The bat is $10 more expensive than the ball.
> How much does the ball cost?
> (One second of thinking music)

If you are like most people, you said the ball cost $1.
Now do the sum again in five or 10 seconds:

> A bat and a ball together cost $11.
> The bat is $10 more expensive than the ball.
> How much does the ball cost?
> (Much more thinking music)

This time, you probably came up with the (correct) answer that the bat costs $10.50 and the ball costs 50 cents.

The first time you did this, you used quick System 1 thinking, even though it probably gave you an answer that just a few seconds' thought would have shown you was wrong. The second time you used your System 2 thinking.

It is worth saying (and we are not 100 per cent sure Kahneman would agree) that we shouldn't always just let System 2 rationality rule. Going with your gut is not just a jumped-up energy saving choice – for example, when choosing which of two employers to work for after being interviewed by them both, sophisticated work on body language, emotions and non-verbal cues has been informing your thinking without you being consciously aware of it. Your mind can serve up this data as 'my gut tells me that this employer is dodgy'. Studies examining firefighters and similar professions show they use their years of experience to make quick decisions that might look like gut decisions but are more likely the hardwired accumulation of all their expertise.

Let's look at some of the cognitive biases more closely.

THE RESEMBLANCE BIAS AND 'LESS IS MORE'

Imagine a man – let's call him Eugene. Picture him at a party. He is the guy hanging away from the main action or in the kitchen. When girls talk to him, he stutters and blushes. He prefers to sit at home or in small groups without the pressure of being funny in front of lots of people. However, if you get to know him, he's really helpful. Once you are a friend, he will go all out for you. He is curious about all sorts of things and loves a good story. You should see his bedroom – it's very tidy, his clothes are carefully folded and his stuff is lined up neatly on his desk. He loves detail, and enjoys comprehensive conversations about the things he is interested in. But don't think he is self-obsessed – he also likes deep conversations about what you're interested in.

Do you think that Eugene is more likely to be a farmer or a librarian?

It is actually more likely that Eugene is a farmer. (We wrote and italicised the word '*librarian*' on this line so that if your eyes flicked down earlier, you saw both words – farmer and librarian.)

Eugene being a farmer is counterintuitive. And the reason he is more likely to be a farmer is because there are 20 times more farmers than librarians in the population. This means that if you pick a tidy, shy, detail-oriented person at random, they are much more likely to be a farmer.

But studies show most people choose the wrong answer. This is because they rely on the 'resemblance' in the character description. The character description made them imagine a neat and buttoned up librarian-type cliché rather than a burly farmer cliché. They didn't think about the statistical base rate of how many people work in each job.

Next, let's engage in another activity just like one in Kahneman's *Thinking, Fast and Slow*. Imagine Monica. Monica is 21. She is very bright and speaks her mind whenever she can. She wrote lots of articles for her school newspaper and now writes for her university paper, particularly about the environment. If you start an argument with her, be prepared to talk for a good hour. Her parents don't have a lot of money, and she is putting herself through university. On the weekends she loves bushwalking.

Rate the following from most (1) to least (5) likely:

a) Monica has a part-time job at McDonald's.
b) Monica is single now but had a boyfriend when she was at school.
c) Monica has a pet dog and dark hair.
d) Monica campaigns against climate change and has a part-time job at McDonald's.
e) Monica catches public transport to university each day.

It is hard to do when you know so little about Monica. It is also hard because this Monica is fictional.

Now your rankings don't matter so much except for one big thing. However you ranked them, a) has to be ranked higher than d).

Why?

It is logically impossible for a) to be less likely than d). This is because every single person in d) (McDonald's workers who campaign against climate change) also has to be in category a) (McDonald's workers) in the first place.

If you got this wrong, you are in good company. Ninety per cent of undergraduates who took this test got it wrong too. If you got it right, congratulations.

What is going on here? The way we described Monica made her sound like someone who would be interested in climate change. People home in on that description because it is more 'representative' of her than just working at McDonald's. Like Eugene the farmer, the story of what Monica is like counts for more than the iron laws of probability in people's minds.

THE AVAILABILITY CASCADE

When you look at news feeds, full of stories about robberies, attacks and terrorist outrages, it's easy to think the world is a very dangerous place. Even during the coronavirus pandemic in Australia people were much more likely to die of a heart attack than the virus. But news reports at the time did not represent this. People could have been forgiven for thinking coronavirus was the country's leading cause of death by a mile.

This sense of danger from terrorist attacks etc is at least partially your fast brain playing a trick on you. It collects recent stories and strong images to shape your view of the world. It doesn't look at the detail of how likely it is that any of these things will happen to you.

For example, most Americans believe that tornados kill more people than asthma despite the fact that asthma kills 20 times more people than tornados. This is because we can more easily imagine huge, disastrous tornados ripping through a town than people undramatically keeling over with an asthma attack.

This is called 'the availability cascade'. It means people judge events to be more likely if individual examples come to mind regardless of whether the event is statistically more likely.

There are many examples of this. Most people are more likely to believe plane travel is dangerous after they see news that a plane has fallen into the sea, even though plane travel is by far the safest form of travel (it would make more sense to be scared every time you got into a car).

Some people think terrorist attacks are a significant danger in major cities like London, New York or Sydney. But you are much, much, much more likely to get run over in a city than get caught up in a terrorist attack. It's just that we can recall terrorist attacks from the news, whereas it's more difficult to remember the incident when a driver knocked over a woman in a suburban street. People think that Hollywood superstars have more affairs than bricklayers, but this is mainly because few examples of bricklayers' saucy love affairs hit the news.

The availability cascade doesn't just apply to newsworthy events. It can happen more locally too. You are more likely to think stealing is on the rise in your suburb if your neighbour's house is broken into, even if statistics show rates of theft in your suburb going down. If you have two or three business failures or play the stock market badly, you think you are going to keep having failures because recent examples from your own life come to your mind.

Psychologist Norbert Schwarz studied this in the early 1990s. He asked one group to write down two examples of how assertive they were, then rate how assertive they thought they were generally. He asked another group to list 12 examples of how assertive they were, then rate how assertive they thought they were generally. The people who had to list 12 examples rated themselves as less assertive, just because they couldn't think of as many examples – even though many of them wrote five or six examples. The availability effect struck here too.

THE ANCHORING EFFECT

This bias needs help from pictures. Bear with them – they might save you hundreds of thousands of dollars one day.

Start by just thinking about the picture above. Take in the numbers, the shape of the wheel. What might it be like to play the game?

Now look at this jar full of little clips that keep wires in place. Write down how many clips you estimate are in the jar.

The answer is … 500.

Perhaps you guessed 500. However, it is more likely you guessed 150 or 200. This is because you looked at the number 100 moments before as part of the roulette table. Even 200 is closer to the number suggested (100) than the correct answer (500).

If you picked 200 you were affected by the number 100 even though we didn't suggest any connection between the number 100 and the number of clips in the jar. The number 100 didn't even have to be in this book – it could have come up on your phone, or because someone scored a century in the cricket match you were watching, or because the show *The 100* came up on Netflix as you read this page. Nonetheless you would have been affected by it.

This is called 'the anchoring effect'. The first number you see or hear anchors your thinking. Other numbers you see or hear revolve around this one.

Daniel Kahneman revealed some interesting examples of this bias. For example, he rigged up a wheel of fortune so that instead of randomly landing on any number from one to 100, it landed only on the numbers 10 or 65. He went into a series of groups and spun the wheel. In some groups it landed only on 10. In others, it landed only on 65. He asked each group to write down the number on which the wheel stopped. Each group duly wrote down either 10 or 65.

He then asked each group, 'What percentage of nations in the UN come from Africa?'

The people who saw the wheel land on 10 estimated, on average, that Africa had 25 per cent of the nations in the UN. People who saw the wheel land on 65 estimated, on average, that Africa had 45 per cent of the nations in the UN. This is a big difference when you consider that the only difference in the two groups was what looked like a completely random number on a wheel of fortune. It can be a little scary to think our estimates about important numbers can be affected by completely irrelevant other numbers.

How to beat it: In a negotiation about money, be the first to suggest a figure. This could apply to your salary or your offer when you are buying a house. As long as the figure is reasonable and not ridiculous, people will take the anchored number more seriously. When there is a large gap – sometimes hundreds of thousands of dollars – in what can be expected, the person who throws out the first anchor is pretty well placed.

And if anyone asks you about the percentage of African nations in the UN, you won't be tricked. (The answer is 28 per cent – 54 of the 193 countries.)

THE PLANNING FALLACY

Have you ever given yourself two hours to research and write an essay, only to get into it and find you actually need 10 hours? Have you ever started a bathroom renovation that you costed at $25,000, only to find it actually cost $50,000 (and took three months instead of one)?

If so, you have been a victim of the planning fallacy.

This fallacy tells us that people are naturally optimistic in many ways. But this optimism leads us to underestimate how long something is going to take and overestimate how successful it will be.

For example, most startups fail. Even though people know this, most entrepreneurs think their startup will buck the trend and become a wild success (and thank heaven for this, otherwise no innovative new idea or company would ever get off the ground).

Not many novelists say to themselves, 'I am going to spend years slaving on my novel so we can sell five hundred copies then find it in a bargain bin'. Instead, they imagine themselves writing a bestseller or a prize-winning book – even though most novels only sell 1000 or 2000 copies. Similarly, few novelists think, 'There is actually about a one per cent chance this will get published at all'. If they did no one would ever start writing a novel.

Even Daniel Kahneman, who researched these biases, was not immune to the planning fallacy. He and his co-workers decided to write a high school textbook about these biases for the Israeli Ministry of Education. As they started, they all wrote down how long they thought it would take and agreed it would take them about two years. They then looked at the evidence revealed by similar projects. It turned out those books had taken between seven and 10 years (and had a 40 per cent chance of failure). Did they abandon the project? No. How long did it take them? Seven years. To add insult to injury, staff left the Ministry of Education in the meantime and the book was never used.

How to beat it: Combine your own guesses with evidence of other similar projects as you plan, whether it is writing an essay, renovating a bathroom or starting up the next tech giant. Don't confuse your best-case scenario with the most likely scenario. Be realistic … but don't let that put you off either.

THE PRIMING EFFECT

This bias is very similar to the anchoring effect. However, instead of being about numbers, it is about images or other types of outside suggestions. It means our conscious choices and our unconscious actions can all be affected by unrelated material from the outside world.

Let's start with the example of money. A group of people in a research trial were shown sentences containing the word 'money'. As well, Monopoly money was left on a table in the room and computer screens showed an image of money floating in water. The people who saw these images were then given a range of unrelated tests. The results were surprising.

The people who saw images of money relied on themselves more than another group of people who hadn't seen these images. They persisted. They spent twice as long on a hard problem before asking for help. What an admirable bunch.

Less admirable is that the people who saw images of money were less likely to help a (stunt) person who pretended to have trouble with an experimental task. They were also less likely to help an experimenter pick up pencils that had been 'accidentally' dropped. Creeps.

As well, two groups (one money primed, one not) were told they were going to meet a new person and were asked to set out two chairs so they could sit together. The people primed with money images put the chairs apart half as far again (118 cm versus 80 cm) as the non-primed group. It seems that just the image of money can make people more determined but less nice.

There are many similar examples. One experimental group was shown images of old people then walked more slowly into the next room. In another instance, researchers set up an experiment in a university department kitchen. It was an honesty system requiring you to put money in a jar for each cup of coffee you made. You got to choose how much money you put in. For 10 weeks, different pictures were put above the jar. In weeks 2, 4, 6, 8 and 10, pictures of flowers were put above the jar. In weeks 1, 3, 5, 7 and 9, pictures of eyes were put above the jar. Every time the eyes were above the jar, people put more money in. Each time flowers were put above the jar, people put less money in. They were being 'primed' by the image, even though no link was made between the image and the jar

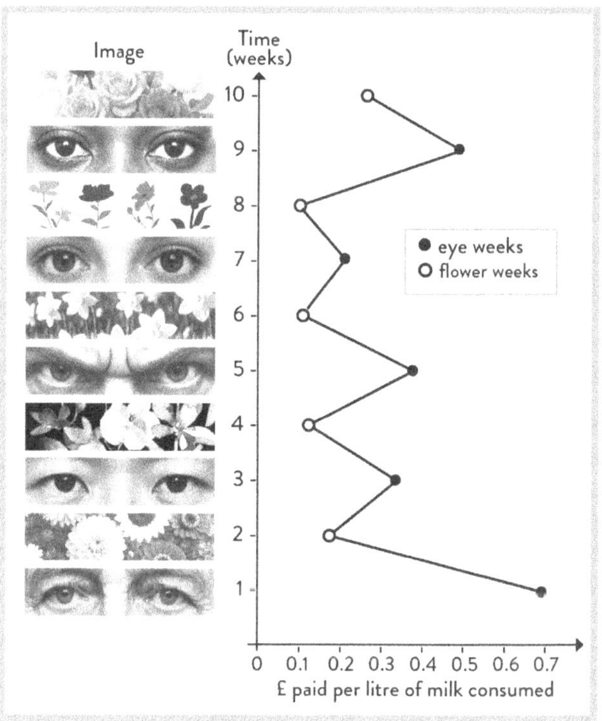

How to beat it: This one is hard to beat. Images are ubiquitous and unconsciously affect our choices. But at least you can be aware of it. Take an audit of what images you see often and what they encourage you to do. For example, go to a mall and look at the images around you. Look around your workplace and/or gym. How might these images affect your choices?

THE LAW OF SMALL NUMBERS

Imagine you want to know whether the latest Marvel movie is good. You either ask half-a-dozen of your best mates or you stop half-a-dozen random people in the streets. Half the people say they liked it and half say it wasn't much good. Then you read on a review site that the same film has an 83 per cent approval rating from audiences and about the same from critics. That's a big difference.

Stopped in the street: 50 per cent
Rotten Tomatoes: 83 per cent

What happened to your survey? If political or other polls were this far out, the pollster would be hounded out of town. Did you ask the wrong people? Did you pick the wrong part of town when you stopped random people in the street? Should you get new, more predictable friends?

No. The problem is that you only asked six people.

If only two more people you interviewed said they liked the latest Marvel movie instead of saying it wasn't much good, you would have been dead on the site's average of 83 per cent. And that's not hard to imagine.

And that's only the start of it. You could skew your numbers in all sorts of ways. If you asked people coming out of a Marvel fan conference, you could easily find five out of six people liked it. If you went to a retirement home and interviewed people in the living room who had just watched *Gone With the Wind*, you might only get one or two.

Similarly, if you wanted to come to your own view about whether the climate was heating up, you wouldn't just take the temperature for two weeks. You might be doing it in summer (oh my god, the planet is burning) or winter (oh my god, the planet is actually cooling). Instead, you would look at thousands upon thousands of data points collected by thousands of actual experts and their interpretation.

That's the law of small numbers. Don't rely on something (particularly a statistic) if the number is small. Small numbers easily lead to more extreme results.

Daniel Kahneman speaks of a particularly striking example of this that he got from statisticians Howard Wainer and Harris Zwerling.[72] He points out that the counties in America where kidney cancer is lowest are in rural, sparsely populated areas of the Midwest. 'Why?' you ask yourself. Could it be the clean living, lower pollution and healthier food of those country farms and towns?

But Kahneman then points out that the counties in America where kidney cancer is the highest are also in rural, sparsely populated areas of the Midwest. Could it be that these areas are poor, have fewer hospitals, and are ridden with alcoholism and opioids?

No. The answer is the law of small numbers again. These counties (out of 3141 counties in America) have by far the lowest number of people. For example, three extra people dying of kidney cancer would make the statistics in a county of 10,000 people skyrocket. By comparison three extra people dying of kidney cancer in New York or Los Angeles (a county of 9.6 million people) is going to make a much smaller difference. Instead of thinking about the numbers, many of our brains jump to tell a story using clichés about rural living.

THE SUNK COST FALLACY

Have you ever struggled to open a packet in the kitchen and just kept going at it? The pack should open, so why isn't it? You keep going and try a couple of different angles to rip it open. There is a pair of scissors in the second drawer, and you could snip the thing open in three seconds but that would be admitting defeat. So instead, you keep trying to tear the pack open. You have determination; you will see this through. And so, 15 seconds later, you finally have it open (and perhaps its contents have exploded across the kitchen, but that's another matter). You have won.

But really, you just lost some time and gained some extra sweeping for the same result. Once it was clear that the package wasn't going to easily open, you had already sunk the cost of trying to open it for a few seconds. So, all that mattered next was whether you were going to take the easy option and use the scissors or keep struggling. But many people think, 'I've already invested the effort; I'm not giving up'.

That's the sunk cost fallacy. It is when a decision or a course of action becomes harder and harder to give up over time, even when it looks like a bad decision in the first place. Humans are more prone to do this than other animals.

The sunk cost fallacy comes in many guises. A friend asks you to invest $10,000 in her mobile phone case business. You do. It doesn't work … yet. She asks you to invest another $20,000. You do. A few weeks later she comes back and says, 'Look, I've hit this unexpected roadblock, but I'm almost there … if you could just give me another $5000'. The project is looking more and more like a failure. But you will probably give her the next $5000 because you can't bear the thought of losing the first $30,000. It probably would have been better to see the first $30,000 as a sunk cost. The only decision you had in front of you at that last moment was whether to invest $5000 on a project that was probably going to fail.

Another guise is when you have a ticket to a concert that, on the day, looks like a dud. Or maybe you don't want to go anymore because you are sick. But you go anyway because you paid for the ticket.

But the money for the ticket went out the door months ago. The only decision on the day is whether you want to go or not. (Of course, if other people are relying on you, that's a different matter.) But if it's only the sunk cost of the ticket making you do something you don't want to do, then you should re-evaluate.

How to beat it: Accept some failures and walk away. Don't throw good time and money after bad. Draw a line and use probabilistic insights about the future to guide your decision. Realise too that advice to 'just stick at it – you will win out in the end' is not always the right advice. Don't become a quitter but do balance the 'stick at it' advice with the 'sunk cost' insight.

THE FRAMING BIAS

The framing bias tells you that you can affect people's choices by the way you present – or frame – your information. That will come as no surprise to many people. It's what all marketing is based on. But this is deeper than finding the right slogans, jingles or ads to promote something. This is about how different choices are made when exactly the same facts are presented in an optimistic or a pessimistic light.

For example, if a salesperson said to you, 'If you take this amazing flight to the moon and back, there is a ninety-nine per cent chance you will live', you are more likely to take it than if the salesperson said, 'If you take this amazing flight to the moon and back, there is a one per cent chance you will die'.

This was tested at Harvard University. The experimenters assembled a group of trainee doctors who were specialising in cancer treatment. In a hypothetical case, the doctors were presented with two choices for treatment – radiation therapy and surgery.

Surgery was undoubtedly the best option. It had a much higher survival rate after five years. But the problem was that if you were going to die after the surgery you were going to do it much sooner – 10 per cent of people died immediately after the surgery. If you could get over that hump, then your long-term survival was much better. (With radiation, 20 or 30 per cent of people died within a year or two.)

But what the doctors chose for their patients was all in the way the same choice was framed.

All of them were given the same statistics for the treatment. Then the surgery was described to half the doctors as 'The one-month survival rate is ninety per cent'. Eighty-four per cent of these doctors chose the surgery option.

The description of the surgery given to the other half of the doctors was: 'There is a ten per cent mortality rate in the first month'. Only 50 per cent of those doctors chose the surgery option.

This is unbelievable stuff. It's the same statistic, just written differently. And it's not as if you are choosing which restaurant to go to, or which deodorant to use – these are life and death decisions.

And this isn't just your average patient being conned; it's a group of trained doctors. Cancer doctors. From Harvard University. But for many, their brains and years of training went out the window when faced with a statistic framed in different ways.

Framing bias is real, powerful and slightly frightening.

How to beat it: It's quite hard. If many cancer doctors can't do it, what chance do we have? But at least we can be on the lookout.

When making a choice, frame it in a variety of ways and consider all of them. For example, when making an investment, think 'I judge that there is a seventy per cent chance I will make a substantial amount on top of my money and there is a fifteen per cent chance I will lose a substantial amount of my money'. Don't just think about the gain or the loss.

When looking at political events, look at the numbers more than the word descriptions. 'Labor almost certain to win the next election' makes you think Labor is basically going to win the next election. However, the same information presented as 'Labor an 85 per cent chance to win the next election' still makes it clear there is a 15 per cent chance the Liberal Party will win the election. That's the same chance as rolling a six on a die, which can easily happen with each throw.

When looking at the percentage chance that something will happen, try to boil it down to the statistics using few emotive words – 'live', 'die', 'make', 'lose' – peppered around as you can. This can be hard. We are story-seeking creatures and most of us like sentences more than numbers.

THE BIKE SHED EFFECT

This bias was coined by historian Cyril Northcote Parkinson in the late 1950s. He didn't use psych tests and years of experimentation. Instead, he crystallised something many people know to be true – that the amount of time people spend making a decision is often in inverse proportion to how important the decision is. In other words, the more important the decision is, the less time people spend making it. He calls it the 'law of triviality'.[73]

He illustrates this with a fictional story about a finance committee that has to approve three different spends.

The first is for a $100 million atomic reactor. Someone suggests a completely different design, but no one wants to accept it because they are not experts in atomic power. It goes through.

The second decision is for a $50,000 bike shed. They debate whether the roof should be aluminium or track shed synthetic. They also discuss how many people would use it and the virtue of using bikes. It is approved.

The third decision is for a $5000 coffee machine for the staff. It is quite expensive for a coffee machine. But it is important for staff morale, so they eventually decide to spend the extra money.

How long does each decision take? The atomic reactor takes 15 minutes, the bike shed 25 minutes and the coffee machine half an hour. A quarter of an hour for a $100 million spend and twice that time for $5000?

Why? It's a fictional example, but everyone knows about coffee so everyone has an opinion. No one wants to challenge the experts in a complicated area. This all adds up to the most time being spent on the least important thing.

That's the bike shed effect.

How to beat it: When you are procrastinating or talking about a decision, ask yourself, 'How important is this decision? Is it worth this amount of time?' It can also be helpful to ask, 'What's the worst thing that can happen if I make a wrong small decision?' (for example, if you end up eating at a Thai restaurant instead of an Indian one after a 10-minute discussion about where to eat).

Also, spot the big decisions (what job to take, what city to live in, whether to have children with that person) in advance and deliberate over them properly. Don't approve a $100 million atomic reactor in 15 minutes.

REGRET BIAS

Let's start with two scenarios.

In the first, you have been exposed to 'rabid racoon' disease. There is a one in 1000 chance you will catch it. If you do, you will cough, splutter, run around like a racoon for 30 seconds then fall over dead. But there is a vaccination for it. How much will you pay for the vaccine?

Decide on a specific number before you move on to the next question. Write it down.

Now imagine you have been asked to participate in a program that will expose you to the rabid racoon disease and a number of different vaccines. There is a one in 1000 chance that you will cough, splutter, run around like a racoon for 30 seconds then fall over dead. How much would you expect to be paid to agree to participate in this program?

Think that number up or write it down.

Probably your second number is more, even though your chance of dying of the disease each time is exactly the same. In a study done by behavioural economist Richard Thaler, people typically wanted to be paid 50 times more to join the test than to buy the vaccine. So, someone who wouldn't pay more than $10,000 for a vaccine would need to receive $500,000 to join the test.

Bizarre, right? It's called regret bias. When people act and lose, their regret is much greater than if they fail to act then lose. Regret bias is a powerful tool that stops people from acting in their own best interests.

How to beat it: Ask yourself whether you are at most risk from holding on to an investment or changing it and investing in something else (this doesn't mean chopping and changing every day).

Ask whether you would hold off from changing your life insurance or bank because it is easier to do nothing and regret than act to change and potentially regret.

Accept that making a decision and taking a loss might be better than sitting inertly and taking a loss. This might be true about asking someone out (and being rejected) or breaking up with them. Sometimes it is better to 'take a plunge' or 'cut and run'. In both cases, action wins over inaction.

THE ILLUSION OF VALIDITY

This bias essentially says that many people overestimate their own 'expert judgement' in an area. They think they have the experience and skills to pick the best candidate for a job or the best investment. But often their decisions are no better than average. It would have been better to rely on data or statistics instead.

Daniel Kahneman uses an example in which he was tasked with choosing army recruits for promotion. The success rate was not much better than if he had picked random people. Nonetheless, another set of recruits was chosen the next year using the same methods. Kahneman also has examples of expert investment advisers being right about as often as a good computer algorithm (and this was long before AI).

The illusion of validity explains why approximately three quarters of people think they are better-than-average drivers.[74] It also explains why 18-year-olds think they are good drivers despite their limited experience on the road.

There are exceptions to this rule: firefighters, for example. Through repeated practice they have developed snap judgments almost akin to 'muscle' memory to respond to different and new situations – particularly sudden danger. This is also true of when you tap the brake on your car almost unconsciously when there is a situation up ahead.

How to beat it: Remember that your expertise often isn't as expert and reliable as you think. Be open to what statistics and data tell you, even if you don't like it much.

THE CONFIRMATION BIAS CLUSTER

This bias is possibly the most persistent and striking of biases. It is the progenitor of several other biases too, among them the 'halo effect'. This bias happens everywhere: where you choose to eat, what politicians you approve of, what friends you like and whether your husband or wife is absolutely fantastic or driving you bat-crazy.

Confirmation bias demonstrates that once you have decided something, you pay too much attention to evidence that tells you you're right and not enough attention to evidence that tells you you're wrong. You go for the confirming information time after time.

Think about McDonald's coffee. If you decide it's actually fine for a drive-through, you will notice all the good coffees, and think of the bad ones as exceptions. On the other hand, if you decide you don't like McCafé coffees you will probably notice each sub-par coffee and downplay any good ones.

Similarly, once you decide you support a political party, you are more likely to approve of the people in its ministry and disapprove of the people in the other party's ministry. You might be negative when someone on the other side does something wrong (for example, is drunk at a late-night session in parliament) but play it down when someone on your side does the same thing. You go looking for incidents that confirm your original choice.

Likewise, once you have decided on a position (for example, taxation is too low) you will be most open to arguments about why taxation should be higher, how greedy mega-corporations avoid tax and how tax is the glue that holds society together. You will also be open to examples of your tax dollar working well for you. You will be more likely be to be dismissive of arguments about why taxation might be too high and believe they are pushed by selfish oligarchs. If you believe taxation is too high, arguments about government waste and the motivating effect of people striving to earn and keep their own money will fall like manna from heaven to your ears. Confirmation bias will keep you marking up arguments for positions you agree with and marking down arguments for positions you disagree with. Even reading this will hardly stop you – you will be lucky if it even slows you down.

This is linked to the halo effect, a bias identified from work done by psychologist Solomon Asch. To understand the halo effect, let's have look at Alan and Ben. Read their characteristics slowly then decide who you would like better.

Alan: Intelligent. Industrious and impulsive. Critical, stubborn and envious.

Ben: Envious. Stubborn and critical. Impulsive, industrious and intelligent.

Most people like Alan better. They read that he is intelligent first, and then industrious. It sounds good. Alan sounds good to work with and good to work for. By the time you get to the stubborn and critical, you think of those features as part of the cost of being industrious. By the time you get to 'envious' you might just shrug your shoulders and think, 'Oh well, you have to take the rough with the smooth'.

Ben, on the other hand, sounds like a jerk from the outset. Not only is he envious, he is stubborn – a toxic combination. Critical too. By the time you read that he is industrious and intelligent you could well be thinking, 'Who cares – it doesn't make me want to go near him'. Indeed, his intelligence might just make him more dangerous.

Yet of course they are the same features in reverse order.

This is the 'halo effect'. Once you start liking someone, you like more and more things they do. This can include unrelated features such as their voice or their looks. You then might start making positive conclusions about totally different elements of their character such as how generous they are, or what they think about an issue that is important to you.

Think about someone you already don't like. Now think about how you view them from day to day. Every time they do something you don't like, you may well think to yourself, 'There they go again, I am so right'. However, if they do something that is different to what you think, you probably tend to dismiss it, downplay it or make excuses for it: 'That jerk at work just went out and got me a cup of coffee and a donut. They are about to backstab me or get me to do a heap of work for them.' It is not impossible that the jerk is indeed about to backstab you with your coffee still warm, but it is more likely to be the reverse halo effect at play and they are just being nice.

WHAT YOU SEE IS ALL THERE IS

Now to the last related bias in this insidious little cluster: 'What you see is all there is'.

To get your head around this, think about the leader of a country, Dr Patel.

Dr Patel is intelligent and strong.

Would you say that Dr Patel is a good leader?

Probably you said, 'Yes.'

Now let's try it again.

Dr Patel is intelligent and strong. Dr Patel is corrupt and cruel.

Would you say that Dr Patel is a good leader?

This time you probably said, 'No.'

This is slightly different to the halo effect bias. In this case, you made a judgement on the basis of only a little information (intelligence and strength). When you got more information (corruption and cruelty) you realised your first judgement was probably wrong. But the key factor is that many people don't look for further information. They have their view, and they will stick with it. What they see is all there is.

So, what actually happens? Your System 1 brain wants to jump to a conclusion. It says, 'Okay, we have enough information. What you see is all there is. Let's get on with it.' Your System 2 brain might have wanted to slow the conclusion down, but your System 1 brain didn't want to do the work.

This is very problematic when you consider many current affairs. People who just get one side of an argument often don't *want* more information. They have their conclusion, and they don't want to hear anything that disturbs it. Unfortunately, most people who have only heard one side of an argument are more confident about their decisions and conclusions than people who have heard out both sides and thus have better information.

Even more problematic is that some people on extreme sides of the political spectrum will put their political allegiance over their ability to accept facts. If the political party someone passionately believes in tells them something 'factual' and is then proved wrong, many people are more likely to believe the incorrect fact even more strongly. People will change their view of reality before they change their political conviction.

How to beat it: This is an important one. When you think you are about to make a judgement, ask yourself if you should get extra information or different perspectives. Ask yourself, 'Would making the decision now be jumping to conclusions?' You can't use this to put off a decision forever, but taking a pause and coming to a deliberative position informed by lots of good information will make you a better friend, student, partner, voter, employee and employer.

Also, actively seek out the other side of an argument. You don't have to agree with it, but put your own arguments through the wringer of the opposite point of view. Read a reputable news site that has a different political leaning to you – and not just to scoff at it. Probe people who have different points of view to see what you can learn from them, and not just so that you can convince them that you have been right the whole time.

PEAK END BIAS

The best way of explaining peak end bias is to look at a bizarre experiment which would never get past an ethics board today. Medical scientist Don Redelmeier and Daniel Kahneman created it.

They took 154 people who were having colonoscopies (a medical procedure where a tube with a camera is inserted into a patient's rectum so doctors can see the patient's large bowel). These operations are now done under anaesthetic so there is little or no pain.

But this is now, not then. Then there was pain. Redelmeier asked the patients every 60 seconds how much pain they were feeling from 0 (no pain) to 10 (intolerable pain). This is one example of what patient A (let's call him Adam) reported:

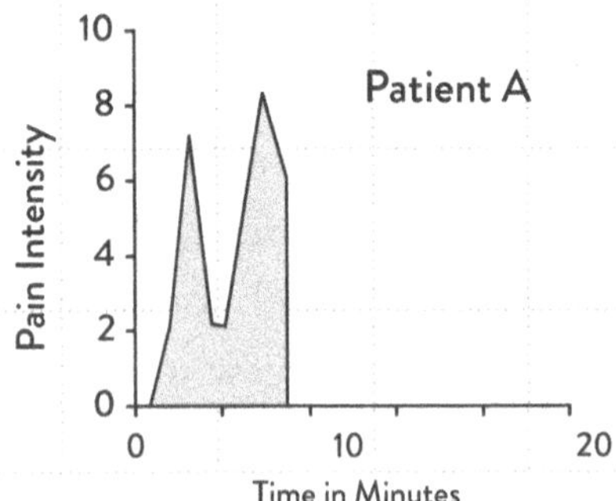

The operation went for eight or nine minutes (the horizontal line) and Adam reported pain from a low of 2 to a high of 8 out of 10 (the vertical line).

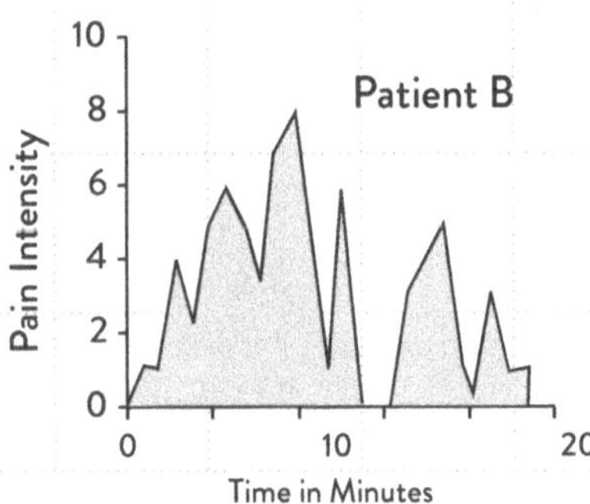

Then with patient B – let's call him Ben – and 77 other patients, they artificially extended the procedure even though the doctors were finished. They basically just kept jiggling the camera so that the patient kept feeling and recording pain. You can see that for Ben, the operation went for 24 minutes instead of eight and he felt pain of up to 5 out of 10 towards the end.

Ben clearly felt more pain than Adam. It was just as bad in the worst bits (highs of 8 out of 10) and Ben's went for almost three times as long.

But when they asked the patients about their pain levels, it was Adam who said there had been more pain. Ben said there had been less pain, even though he had suffered more. This pattern was repeated time and time again with the 154 patients they tested.

These results were repeated in a variety of other tests over the years. In one study, people stuck their hands in ice cold water for a few minutes at a time. In that test, people who had their hands in the ice cold water for longer, but had a tiny bit of warm water put in the bowl at the end, reported less overall pain.

So, what is going on?

The answer is that people mainly remember an experience by what happened towards the end. For the patients having a colonoscopy, the final few minutes really mattered for remembering. Because that part of the experience wasn't so bad (5 out of 10 pain), this was what the patients mainly remembered. This is 'peak end bias'.

Our 'remembering' self recalls things quite differently to our 'experiencing' self. Our remembering self goes through and edits what is happening.

This has a few consequences. To recall a holiday pleasantly, it matters less how many days it went for and more about what you did in the last few days (so perhaps four days in a resort is just as good as 10, and a lot cheaper). When you recall a movie you watched, you will think more about the last 15 minutes than the first 15 minutes. And it raises a question: should hospitals unnecessarily lengthen painful procedures so that patients will remember less pain?

How to beat it: Train your brain to reflect on the whole experience, not just the end of it. Focus on remembering what happened in the middle, which was just as likely to have been the best part. It's another reason to try to get the worst part of something over first – you will remember it less. Eat dessert last.

A NOTE ON ALL THE BIASES

It is uncomfortable to think about how close we are to the hunter-gatherer of hundreds of thousands of years ago, always on the lookout for lunch and always on guard against becoming it.

On one hand it is impossible to rationally commit to never falling for these unconscious biases, for one obvious reason. Even if we become aware of the biases, they will still whir away in the back of our mind, muscling their way into our decisions and insinuating their way into our views. It can be sobering, but it doesn't have to be dispiriting.

Humanity's determined use of reason globally has allowed us to uncover all these cognitive biases. It shows that we can use tried and tested critical thinking principles to uncover error. We can be proud of the fact that we are at least aware of the biases, in a way that previous generations and centuries weren't. Awareness of confirmation bias, availability cascades and other biases allows us to make better public policy for the good of everyone – and we can bet they are being used more now than they were back in the Dark Ages or even the start of last century. We have a great deal to thank Daniel Kahneman and his fellow researchers for.

At a personal level, being aware of the biases can at least limit how often we fall into them. This awareness will – not always, but often – allow us to make better decisions. Regression to the mean will help us understand our test scores a bit more. Confirmation bias will limit our chance of being sucked into a news bubble of fury and agreement. The anchoring effect might help us pay less for a house. Regret bias could help us pay less for insurance or persuade us not to keep a bad investment. Finally, and perhaps most significantly, peak end bias will almost certainly ensure we check the conditions before going to have a colonoscopy.

CHAPTER 5
THINKING FALLACIES OF RELEVANCE

Fallacies are the pernicious weeds of critical thinking. They are reasoning that is invalid or simply chokes up proper thinking. The problem is that, superficially, fallacies often look quite unobtrusive, so they can be hard to spot or uproot. People sow them into their arguments all the time and often win because of them. However, part of good thinking is to be on the lookout for fallacies and not be taken in by them. You should also make sure you don't inadvertently use them yourself and convince yourself of weak arguments.

Like real weeds, there are many, many types of fallacies. You could dive deep into them and not be seen for weeks. They also overlap substantially. We have selected some of the most common. The first group covers 'fallacies of relevance' – when irrelevant material is added to an argument. The second group covers 'fallacies of presumption' – when something unproven or wrong is embedded or hidden in the argument, often as an assumption. Fallacies of presumption are often harder to spot (see page 179).

Before you get into them, we have two warnings.

Firstly, these are not the daily stuff of thinking critically. You can think well, decide thoughtfully and use core procedures like 'premise/conclusion/inference/assumption' without really diving into fallacies. Indeed, fallacies only emerge when things start to go wrong. Nonetheless, you will probably recognise most of these reasoning flaws immediately because you have seen them so often. At least now you will have pithy names for them.

Secondly, strive to be a fair-minded thinker as well as a strong one. Fallacies could be deliberately used to convince other people of nonsense to sway their judgement. You could make people believe dreadful arguments and conclusions. You could convince others to make weaker and worse decisions. Remember, thinking is also about character – indeed, it could well be about character first and foremost (see chapter eight.) If you want to have intellectual courage, integrity and humility, knowing about fallacies should mean uprooting them where you find them, not sowing them.

ARGUMENT FROM FALSE AUTHORITY

As we eat our sugary breakfast cereal (recommended by the entire Australian cricket team), wash it down with a protein shake (Ironman food – they say they eat it every morning), slip into our LeBron sneakers (sure, they cost twice as much as other sneakers, but LeBron James knows all about how to make a sneaker) then pop a few dietary supplement tablets recommended by an online influencer (trained in nothing at all), it's clear that arguments from false authority are pervasive.

The Latin term for 'arguments from false authority' is 'ad verecundiam'. It was first coined back in the seventeenth century by English philosopher John Locke.[75] There are different types of argument from false authority. Obviously, we fell for a form of celebrity endorsement in our earlier breakfast preparations – being an expert in cricket, running or basketball does not make someone an expert in nutrition. Another form is an expert supporting an argument outside their field. Albert Einstein is a classic example – despite being a physicist he is often quoted about education, philosophy, religion and any number of other subjects outside physics.

Then there is the unidentified expert. You have probably heard a friend say, 'Researchers agree the current education model is busted', or 'The experts reckon we are about to head into a quarter of negative growth'. Without the actual names of any of these experts, the claims ring hollow. There is also an invulnerable expert – the national leader of an authoritarian state who can't be disputed or the deity who must be believed in all things without any recourse to reason.

Not relying on the assertions of others prompts you to find out for yourself – to look up facts, find evidence, construct arguments and use your own critical reasoning faculties. It is one of the things our free and liberal society, working properly, does best.

However (and this matters) ...

It is usually fine to substantially trust the opinions of experts in their own fields. This is a **reasonable argument from authority**. An expert is someone with a lot of training and experience in a particular area. They usually know more than the leaders and the general population, and it is wiser (and more efficient) to trust them than it is to get a degree in the same subject yourself. A traffic consultant knows more about the effective placement of traffic lights than the average member of the public. An air traffic controller knows more about managing flights out of an airport than most. If several doctors told you that you had a heart problem you wouldn't say, 'Well, I feel fine, so I must be okay' or 'Well, five of my mates told me I don't have heart problems, so it's even'. You'd back the experts.

This is also the case with contentious areas such as climate science. Science historian Naomi Oreskes published a famous report in 2004 that looked at 928 articles about climate published in the previous 20 years. About 700 of their summaries explicitly or implicitly agreed that climate change was a phenomenon and about 200 didn't have an opinion. None said climate change was not a phenomenon.[76] With a scientific consensus like this, it is not unreasonable to say, 'Look, my reading of the newspapers does not make me a climate expert so I am going to accept what the vast majority of scientific experts are telling me'.

It does not have to be complete and total faith. There is rarely consensus in any expert field – science, medicine, economics, law – and you sometimes have to juggle conflicting expert opinions. Astronomer and scientist Carl Sagan said, 'One of the great commandments of science is "Mistrust arguments from authority." (Scientists, being primates, and thus given to dominance hierarchies, of course do not always follow this commandment.)'[77] However, baked into the discipline of science is a process in which you check, distrust, find conflicting opinions and check again. And this process is better than most people or organisations.

In a world where you can find a hundred different opinions, factoids and internet rants about every subject under the sun, the need to rely on substantial authority becomes more important than ever.

Good luck. Don't rely on false or misleading authorities, and pay proper attention to experts in their own field. Use your best judgement to tell the difference. It might be difficult, but it is much better than falling prey to whatever misinformation comes your way.

TRY IT OUT

At first glance, which of these examples look more like argument from false authority, and which look reasonable?

- The prime minister and the opposition leader say we need to increase military spending to counter a new geopolitical world.
- 'Mitigating the risk of extinction from AI should be a global priority alongside other societal-scale risks, such as pandemics and nuclear war' reads a one-sentence statement released by the Center for AI Safety, a nonprofit organisation. The open letter was signed by more than 350 executives, researchers and engineers working in AI.
- Chris Hemsworth recommends NRMA car insurance and says it is the best in town.
- After an examination in her office, your GP tells you that you probably have pancreatic cancer and three months to live.
- Billie Eilish says streaming music services seriously increase the amount of royalties that musicians receive.

THE EXCLUDED MIDDLE

This is one of the most significant fallacies around. It leads to political extremism, global wars and people being mean to their neighbours. If the phrase 'excluded middle' could be heard in workplaces and political corridors as often as 'how was your weekend', the world might be a better, safer place.

The excluded middle occurs when someone suggests that the only alternative to one action or opinion is the opposite action or opinion. If you are not for a war on drugs, then you are all for letting drug lords run the city or you're a drug lover yourself. If you are not 'on the bus' with the new management team at your workplace, you should get off the bus right now. If you don't think Upper Moldova is the new evil empire, you are an Upper Moldovan sympathiser. If you don't fully support Chloe in Year 9 in her fight with the wicked Amy, you are clearly just a buddy of wicked Amy and should go and sit with her instead.

What this obscures is the whole range of positions in the middle. Imagine drawing a line with the two extreme positions of the drug debate at either end (for example, no tolerance versus total acceptance). Then along the spectrum insert a number of middle positions – for example, 'make drugs illegal, but have treatment programs'; 'have heavier punishments for distributors but not for users'; 'make some drugs legal but not others'; 'put some drugs on prescription'. All these positions sit somewhere along the line between zero tolerance and total acceptance. This exposes the original two positions (war on drugs/let drug lords run the city) and shows they are not a binary choice, but instead the two extremes. When you 'exclude the middle' you erase or collapse every (probably more reasonable) solution or idea between them.

When enough of the middle is excluded, a polarised political structure emerges. People have great difficulty compromising or talking to each other. People make fake and unnecessary choices. Reasonable, diplomatic, sensible solutions are thrown into the dumpster fire that political warriors want because those solutions don't anger people or rile them up.

One of the most famous examples of 'excluding the middle' was promoted in the wake of the attacks on the World Trade Center and the Pentagon in the United States in September 2001. On 13 September 2001, Senator Hillary Clinton said, 'Every nation has to either be with us or against us'.[78] President George Bush said, 'Every nation, in every region, now has a decision to make. Either you are with us or you are with the terrorists'.[79] That is a pretty grim option for friendly countries or individuals who want to say, 'Well, we are your good friends, but invading Iraq seems a very problematic idea'. You don't want to be seen as supporting the terrorists, so you might keep your individual or national mouth shut. And so entire armies went to what is now generally regarded as an unnecessary war that cost many lives.

It can happen in more mundane circumstances as well. You think you have to choose between buying new furniture for the living room or going on a holiday. You could choose to go on a cheaper holiday. You could buy cheaper furniture. You could choose to buy the furniture for the living room a piece at a time over a few years. There are lots of intermediate positions.

As you go through life you will see the excluded middle expressed in other ways too. It is part of false dichotomies or false dilemmas. You will see it often in people who have black and white thinking. The section later in this book called 'Going from "either/or" to "both/and" thinking' (see page 219) is a relative of the excluded middle.

TRY IT OUT

Can you think up some 'excluded middle' examples, perspectives or solutions in the following areas?

- For their next holiday, Josie wants to go to mountainous, landlocked Nepal to trek and John wants to go to the Maldives to lie on a beach.
- At school, Nick wants to hang out with both the music and the soccer kids.
- After their initially successful invasion of Australia, the New Zealand government demands total loyalty from the Australian people.
- The rights of a woman and the rights of a foetus in an abortion/reproductive rights debate.

ARGUMENTS FROM EMOTION

It is often fine to use emotion as a significant part of your decisions. If someone says, for example, 'Will you marry me?' and you do not consult your emotions, you may well have a difficult, even torturous, and strangely flat life ahead of you. However, people proposing arguments sometimes aim to manipulate your emotions. You should be wary of both them and their arguments.

The argument from pity: Poor Bill needs this job as a bus driver because he hasn't had a job for 12 months, his family is hungry, his terrible eyesight gets him down, he has clinical depression from PTSD after witnessing a robbery and he can barely exercise because of his amputated leg. We feel for Bill. But we do not want him driving us or our kids home on a bus. Being swayed by pity can lead to poor judgement calls in employment, public affairs, romance and more.

Defence counsel use the argument from pity all the time to get their clients a lighter sentence, and to some extent mitigating factors are relevant. However, a bad upbringing should only go so far for a defendant if they have just robbed every bank in town. Being affected by ice should not make it okay to plough your car into a family of six. Your kids might try arguments from pity now and then too – they can't do their homework because their geography teacher had a stern word with them, or they have a pimple outbreak, or they are upset about the blind, one-legged bus driver who drove them home that afternoon. It's okay to have compassion – and have it in spades – as long as it does not dominate judgement.

The argument from fear: Used by demagogues and wayward teenagers the world over, an argument from fear begins with the arguer projecting a (often unfounded) concern into the cinema of our minds, then amplifying this fear to influence a decision. Fear can be used as an argument against travel, immigration, moving from one city to another or change of almost any sort. The argument from fear should be distinguished from a quite reasonable argument from adverse consequences. For example, saying, 'Don't lean too far over the handrail of this ocean liner because you might fall into the ocean' is not an argument from fear but a proper caution.

TRY IT OUT

Make up an example of argument from emotion for the following situations:

- an opposition politician trying to stop mobile phone towers on the basis that they could cause cancer
- stopping a bank from raising the interest rates on mortgages
- being underage at your end-of-school celebration and not getting into a nightclub
- stopping the war with Upper Moldova after it has dragged on for three decades.

ATTACKING THE PERSON

This happens when instead of attacking a person's argument you attack them personally. You try to sully their character, their trustworthiness or their reliability so that you do not have to tackle the actual merits of their argument. As well as being a fallacy, it is mean spirited. A really fair-minded thinker would not stoop to it. Its Latin term is 'ad hominem'.

The most obvious version is a direct attack that is completely unrelated to what the person is talking about: 'Mitch wants the local government to stop cutting down the trees on the pavement. But he brays like a horse, cheats on his tax and smells.' If you can impugn someone's character enough, any policy they support looks less solid. Australia's very wealthy former Prime Minister Malcolm Turnbull was sometimes criticised as being too rich and out of touch regardless of what policy he proposed. But genuine character faults do not make a person's views about everything suspect. Philosophy professor George Wrisley, in his book *Bad Arguments*, uses the case of the American General David Petraeus, who gave classified documents to a reporter he was having an affair with. This act is bad, but it probably did not affect his expert judgement about whether ISIS was a threat. His infidelity should not have been used to discard his expertise on what was a critical issue at the time.[80]

People often attack someone personally because they think that person has a bias or vested interest in a decision. But a vested interest does not necessarily disqualify them. It is not okay to accuse someone of loving Toyotas if they are a car salesman trying to sell you a Toyota (it might be worse if they *didn't* like Toyotas). Similarly, showing how someone can personally profit from a decision they are proposing doesn't necessarily make the decision bad: 'You want higher wages for nurses – no wonder; you are a nurse'.

On many occasions, pointing out a personal interest is relevant and is not an ad hominem argument. Billionaires who propose cuts to the highest rate of tax could have their wealth highlighted. George Wrisley uses the example of a Monsanto company executive who argues that Monsanto's genetically modified seed crop is safe because of studies A, B and C. The executive has bias – they want the seed to be approved – and they could be criticised for this. But they might also be right – the seed could be brilliant and safe. You would have to look carefully at the studies before deciding whether this is a bad use of the ad hominem argument.

Pointing out hypocrisy can be a good or a bad use of the ad hominem argument. If somebody is preaching the morality of monogamy and also cheating on their husband with the local football team, it would be okay to bring up their personal life. Sometimes, though, this can be used as an excuse to sully important messages. A 14-year-old child told by their parent not to vape might say, 'But *you* smoke', and the parent could still have validity if they are trying to warn the child about mistakes they have made themselves.

Another form of 'ad hominem' is what is called 'tu quoque'. It basically means 'you too'. It is a type of tit-for-tat argument. One person calls another a hypocrite for advocating random breath testing after being caught speeding. The other person could say, 'Look who's talking – I saw you speeding down the main street just last week'. In both cases it's ad hominem – the issue of drunk driving is not the same as speeding. But the second person, rather than point out the first person's personal attack, has doubled down with an attack of their own.

In our sound-bitey, aggressive and often mean-spirited online and political climate, ad hominem attacks are used frequently. A few have substance. However, a lot are merely noise that you will hopefully be able to filter out.

TRY IT OUT

Are the following examples of 'attacking the person', and how convincing are they?

- We, the Government of South Braskville, reject Australia's criticism that we have tortured and killed 75 per cent of our population. What a bunch of hypocrites – look at their own human rights record. How dare they even speak to us.
- A senator from Victoria says more people should get higher education, but what would she know? She never got past Year 12.
- Our neighbour says we should stop immigration. But he is a bigot who has said dozens of racist things about Chinese and Indian people to us over the last year.
- John says I should stand tall – what an idiot, he's only 162 cm himself.

STRAW MEN, WEAK MEN, HOLLOW MEN AND UNFAIR EXTENSION

A straw man is literally a dummy made of straw used for target practice. A **straw man** argument happens when someone refuting an argument does something very tricky – they replace the real argument with a different, easier argument – one 'made of straw'. They then shoot down that argument instead. It is a fairly low move but it works most of the time.

For example, imagine children say to their parents, 'We want to use less plastic, stop using the clothes dryer, recycle more and get solar panels'. Now imagine the parents reply, 'Fine, you want to get all environmentally aware, but you're not even aware of what a mess you leave the kitchen all the time. Start with our home environment and start pulling your weight around here.' The family then get into an argument about whether the kids do their share of housework and clean up after themselves.

The parents have shifted the argument. They changed the meaning of environment from 'world environment' to 'kitchen environment' and switched 'reduce energy consumption' to 'be tidy'. This is the straw man in action.

A very famous and often quoted political example is Richard Nixon when he was running for Vice President of the United States in 1952. He was accused of misappropriating $18,000 of campaign funds for personal use. His reply to the press (known as the Checkers speech) climaxed with this statement:

> *We did get something, a gift, after the election. A man down in Texas heard Pat on the radio mention the fact that our two youngsters would like to have a dog. And believe it or not, the day before we left on this campaign trip we got a message from Union Station in*

> *Baltimore, saying they had a package for us. We went down to get it. You know what it was? It was a little cocker spaniel dog in a crate that he'd sent all the way from Texas, black and white, spotted. And our little girl Tricia, the six year old, named it 'Checkers'. And you know, the kids, like all kids, love the dog, and I just want to say this, right now, that regardless of what they say about it, we're gonna keep it.*[81]

The dog was not campaign funds. No one was accusing him of misappropriating poor old Checkers. In fact, the dog arrived after the election in question. However, this straw man is what was remembered from the speech (and to be fair, the speech did also contain other, more relevant details). Nixon and Eisenhower were elected in a landslide.

Connected to the straw man fallacy is the **weak man** argument where you just pick on the weakest of an opponent's five or six arguments. This one is not as problematic – after all, your opponent really did make those argument. But effective counterarguments should go after the strongest arguments as well as the weakest ones.

Completing our collection of dodgy men is the **hollow man**. This happens when someone makes up a person, makes up their arguments, then attacks those fictitious arguments. For example, 'Lefties secretly just want the government to walk through their front door and take over every aspect of their lives. Goodbye to the everyday freedoms we take for granted.' But which leftie said this? None. You'd be hard pressed to find a leftie who thought that government should (even metaphorically) walk into their house and dictate whether to have beef or chicken for dinner. But arguing – well, vilifying actually – is so much easier when you can make up both the argument and the person who made it.

Closely linked to the straw man is **unfair extension**. In the example on the previous page about the children wanting to be more environmental, imagine the parents' response was, 'Fine, sounds like you want to give up all mod cons. Why don't we just go and live in a cave?' Firstly, the kids said, 'We want to *reduce* our energy and plastic consumption'. The parents extended that argument to 'We want to *give up* energy and plastic' – which the kids don't. In fact, it was a double sneak. The parents also turned 'some' mod cons (ie the clothes dryer) into 'all' mod cons. Unfair extension has been used by both sides of the environment debate over the years: an environmentally conscious person is cast as an extremist loon; people who want to reliably turn on an electric light are smeared as proponents of energy that will turn the planet into a coal fired slag heap (okay, maybe that's a bit of unfair extension of our own).

TRY IT OUT

Create straw man or unfair extension arguments about the following:

- evangelicals or atheists
- feminists
- people who want bike lanes
- people who want to rapidly end the mining of fossil fuels.

FALSE ANALOGY

False analogies can be a fun way to confound your friends – or perhaps convert them into mere acquaintances. They are superficially appealing and vivid: 'Heating up the Earth is like heating up a room – eventually you can just turn on the air conditioner' or 'You need a licence to drive a car so why don't you need a licence to be a parent?'

For a millisecond these arguments have the comfortable ring of truth … before you work out there's something very wrong. Heating up the Earth is nothing like heating up a room – the Earth has no air conditioning system we can just flick a switch on. And a society that required licences for parenthood would be a dystopian nightmare (what would you do with parents who didn't get the licence?), unlike the reasonable expectation that you learn how to drive a car before you get onto a road that has other cars.

These examples are both false analogies. A false analogy involves finding two things that have a particular similarity or thing in common (for example, 'heating' in the case of the Earth and a room). Then, because of that similarity, you propose a different similarity that you can't really justify (for example, 'flicking a switch' to turn down the heat). This was famously clarified by philosopher and economist John Stuart Mill in his 1843 book *A System of Logic.*[02]

Not all analogies are bad. A lot of excellent reasoning occurs through analogies, metaphors and comparisons. They work well when the element being compared is the element they have in common. For example, a lot of interesting work has been done on the arguments about abortion by using the analogy of someone waking up one morning to find a violinist attached to their body. Would they have the right to disconnect the violinist? The wheels fall off when, because of one similarity that is true, a whole lot of other similarities that are not true are loaded on.

One of the most famous false analogies is theologian William Paley's 1802 watchmaker analogy. He imagines walking across a heath and stubbing his foot on a stone. When he wonders how the stone came to be there, the answer could be that it was always there. But if he stubbed his foot on a watch, with its wheels and intricate workings, he could not say it had always been there. He would have to say some clever person made it, presumably a watchmaker. So too, when you look at the Earth, with its interweavings and complexity, it too could not have always just been there. Someone or something (in Paley's view, God) must have made it.

But the invention of a mechanical watch is not, as it turns out, like the development of the Earth. The workings of physics, chemistry, geology, evolution, natural selection and an extraordinary amount of time *do* have the capacity to develop the world to where it is. This is not to say that there isn't a God; only that Paley's analogy does not prove that there is.

Analogies – false, weak or strong – can help in deciding your views. For example, people often wonder what responsibility social media has for the racist, bizarre or objectionable material on its platforms. If you use the analogy that social media is like a post office, then it has no responsibility, just as you wouldn't hold the post office responsible if someone sent you a racist letter. If you use the analogy that social media is more like a newsroom, then it has a lot of responsibility – just as you would hold a newsroom responsible if its news anchor said something really racist.

So analogies can clarify your thought, but watch out for the many false analogies. They can lead you to becoming unduly worried, or unduly complacent. Because we are storytelling creatures and love a vivid example, we are often keen to make connections and jumps. But as often as not, the connection is not really there.

TRY IT OUT

How would you rate these analogies out of 10 (1 being very false, 10 being very true)? Why?

- Being addicted to your phone is like being addicted to drugs or gambling – it's almost impossible to stop.
- Driving a car in Sicily is like entering a war zone.
- Writing essays for your university degree is like making sausages from a sausage machine: put all that meaty content in the top of your head and just spit out those sausage-shaped essays.
- Putting food in your body after exercise is like fuelling your car – you need that nutrition to make everything run.

THE GALILEO GAMBIT

Sometimes a person's defence of their own strange arguments can make your brain melt and make it hard to come up with a neat, cooling response. The 'Galileo gambit' will help you take the heat out of their argument in at least a few of these cases.

Firstly, a bit of history: Galileo, in the early seventeenth century, advanced the theory that the Earth went around the sun (it was heliocentric) instead of the sun going around the Earth (it was geocentric). He was reputed to say, 'In questions of science, the authority of a thousand is not worth the humble reasoning of a single individual'.[83] Galileo was forced by the church, which encouraged him by displaying some torture instruments, to recant this. In Galileo's case, he wasn't going against the authority of a thousand scientists, but seventeenth century churchmen who were not using science or applied mathematics. Their medieval view that the sun went around the Earth was unable to be falsified because their ecclesiastical sources asserted it, and it lined up with their everyday experience (the sun went up and down every day). This is why the humble reasoning of one person with scientific evidence on his side ultimately prevailed in this case.

The Galileo gambit happens when someone proposes an idea that goes against all current science (for example, that healing crystals fix cancer) then, when challenged, say, 'Yes, but Galileo was accused by everyone of being wrong too, and he turned out to be right … just like I will be'. The Galileo gambit makes it sound as if criticism of an argument makes the argument more likely to be right. If this argument carried any weight, then every weird, fictional, unsupported argument would be more likely to be right just because it is so weird, fictional and unsupported. Do you want to believe the Earth is flat? Well, go right ahead – they laughed at Galileo too. Do you want to believe the moon landing was faked? You've got Galileo on your side.

Do you want to believe the climate is not heating up against all the available evidence? Go right ahead, you're in the trenches with the great Galileo himself, who also stood up against the existing scientific orthodoxy.

But being accused of being wrong is not evidence that you are right. If a lot of experienced, informed people are accusing you of being wrong, it is pretty good evidence that you are wrong.

Philosophy professor David Kyle Johnson[84] says the Galileo gambit isn't even a good name for the fallacy because Galileo went up against the church, not the scientific consensus. A better name for it would be 'Pasteur's gambit' (because microbiologist Louis Pasteur claimed, against the scientific consensus, that germs caused disease) or 'Wegener's gambit' (because geologist Alfred Wegener proposed, against the scientific consensus, that the continents had drifted into their current positions). But at least science has self-correction in its DNA, and allows for humble reasoning to eventually improve on, or overturn, accepted theories. Scientific theories don't claim to be 100 per cent right – only that more and more evidence for a theory just takes it beyond 'probable' into 'beyond reasonable doubt'.

For every scientist who got it right against the consensus, there are hundreds who got it wrong – they just haven't been remembered by history, precisely because they were wrong. If you have a friend with a lonely, crackpot theory, it is more likely that they are not on the cusp of epochal greatness but instead stand with those whose own lonely crackpot theories are going to the graveyard.

The Galileo gambit also has strong hints of 'unfalsifiability' in it. Nothing can disprove your theory because the more evidence presented *against* your theory, the more noble and courageous you are for standing up for it.

We leave the final words here to the inestimable Carl Sagan from his book *Broca's Brain: Reflections on the Romance of Science*: 'The fact that some geniuses were laughed at does not imply that all who were laughed at were geniuses. They laughed at Columbus, they laughed at Fulton, they laughed at the Wright Brothers. But they also laughed at Bozo the Clown.'[85]

TRY IT OUT

Rank the following statements from the one most to the one least like a Galileo's gambit.

A. We, the mighty Lions rugby team, might be last on the table. People have told us to give up. But that's what they told the Broncos five years ago when they were last, and they ended up in the semi-finals. Watch us roar, starting next week!
B. I say the sun and all the stars revolve around the Earth. Don't believe me? Well, nobody believed Galileo either.
C. You think teaching thinking skills explicitly is a bad thing? Well, that's what they said about explicitly teaching grammar for 50 years – look how right teaching grammar turned out to be.
D. Here is my new field theory to describe reality: you put your five senses on the x axis and the four space/time dimensions on the y axis so you can plot multiple spots on the cartesian planes for holistic experience – for example, height/hearing or time/taste. You say this is ridiculous nonsense? Well, that's what they said about Einstein's theory of relativity.

(We think D, B, C, A, although if you have a different answer, let us know why you are right. After all, nobody believed Galileo at the time either.)

RED HERRINGS

Red herrings are the perfect logical flaw for an easily distracted, goldfish-brained person. Here's a very obvious illustration:

John: Have you been cheating on me? That's immoral.

Jane: Perhaps. But look at this delicious beer I bought you on the way home.

John: Oooh … I love beer.

There was an attempt by John to make an argument. But instead of responding to the issue at hand, Jane diverted and distracted the argument, in this case successfully. Someone as challenged as John perhaps deserves to be cheated on. But red herrings often work.

John: Have you been cheating on me? That's immoral.

Jane: But what is morality? I mean, ethicists have been trying to pin that down for centuries.

John: I think morality is based in our individual cultures.

John is terminally distracted here too. But in both cases Jane has successfully diverted the attention away from John's claim and argument.

The term 'red herring' originated with hunting. Hounds were trained to go after foxes. The trainers would let the fox out, leaving its scent behind. The trainers would then go to where the fox had just been with strong-smelling, pickled fish – red herrings – and drag them on the ground in a different direction to the fox. Some hounds, when released, would be distracted by the scent of the red herring instead of chasing down the fox. These hounds either got retrained or lost their jobs. The better hounds stuck with the original scent through to its sad, foxy conclusion. And so it is with arguments. (Incidentally, if you want to use a red herring as a red herring, all you have to say is that they are not really red – it's the brine and the pickling that turns them that colour.)

Red herrings distract attention and allow people to avoid scrutiny. They can be a form of fake morality:

> Shareholder of food company: Does some of the food we make rely on palm oil grown in deforested regions of the Brazilian rainforest?
>
> Company representative: We are responsible and good people. We focus on many charitable works and we give 20 per cent of our profits to save the South American llama.

Politicians frequently use it to change the subject to something they would prefer to talk about. In fact, they will sometimes be briefed to get their message out regardless of what they are asked:

> Reporter: Do you think you have done enough to alleviate inner city poverty?
>
> Mayor: I am proud of my inner-city record. Crime is down and the beautification of the roads and parks is up. This benefits everyone in the inner city.

The red herring fallacy can also be used to simply attack their opponents (an example of the fallacy of 'attacking the person' – see page 155).

> Reporter: Do you think you have done enough to alleviate inner city poverty?
>
> Mayor: Before you ask that you should look at my opponent's record on inner city poverty when she was the mayor. She didn't give it a thought from one year to the next. Poverty skyrocketed during her tenure.

Whole speeches, issues and campaigns can be red herrings. The film *Wag the Dog* is about a politician who looks like he is going to lose an election, and so invents a fake war. Of course, his popularity goes up.

The best way to avoid the red herring fallacy in your own arguments is simply to answer the question. The best way to avoid being caught by the red herring fallacy is to keep focusing back on the question you wanted an answer to.

TRY IT OUT

Employ 'red herring' arguments to distract people from the actions below (remember to be fair-minded and please don't try them in real life, particularly the third one).

- You have left the kitchen in a mess.
- You have pulled out of going away for a weekend with a friend.
- You just dropped a nuclear bomb on India.
- You have just lost $10,000 gifted by your great aunt by investing in a dubious startup.
- You forgot to buy a colleague a coffee when they have bought you one for the past three days.

THE GENETIC FALLACY

Imagine two scenes. The first is a perfect, snowy Christmas morning. Two delightful children, Joe and Jane, excitedly open their Christmas presents from Santa, which have been hanging from the fireplace. Little Santa baubles hang on the Christmas tree and Father Christmas images gaze down from many of the Christmas cards on the sideboard. Then mean Uncle Greg turns up, perhaps fresh from the local 24/7 pub. 'Christmas presents!' he scoffs to Jane and Joe. 'You shouldn't be getting Christmas presents – it's all a capitalist plot. Don't you realise the modern image of Santa was made up as an advertising ploy by Coke in the 1930s? Look at that red and white get up – just like a Coke can. If you get into presents from Santa, all you are doing is supporting the multinational, capitalist market system as well as evil sugary carbonated drinks.' Joe and Jane burst into tears, discarded wrapping paper strewn around them like a testament to broken dreams, while Joe and Jane's parents carefully steer Uncle Greg off to shower and have a lie down. (Note to younger readers who receive annual visits from Santa: Uncle Greg is incorrect and deluded.)

In the second scene, Uncle Greg is a politician, though not a very good one. Three months later he is exposed by the local newspaper for taking bribes. As he is taken away past the waiting camera crews he cries out, 'Don't trust the media – they have stitched me up. They lie so much they have forgotten how to tell the truth.'

What do these two scenes have in common? In both cases Uncle Greg is committing the 'genetic fallacy', also known as the 'fallacy of origin'. This is where a belief or argument is challenged based on where the argument came from – its origin or genesis. By concentrating on the argument's origin, Uncle Greg can distract us from the substance of the argument itself. In the case of the Christmas argument, it is not a strong argument that kids should not enjoy presents at Christmas because Coke had a go at redesigning Father Christmas's costume nearly a century earlier. In the case of the media, Uncle Greg discrediting the name of the source does not discount the argument or the claims the source makes.

The genetic fallacy can also wrongly be used to support an argument, so it cuts both ways. For example, someone might say, 'I have always believed taxation is a crime, because my father believed taxation was a crime, and his father believed taxation was a crime and his father went to jail for refusing to pay his taxes because he believed taxation was a crime.' This proud family tradition is not much of a reason to believe taxation is a crime. As Kevin Klement says, 'Knowing or trusting the origin of a belief does not assess the validity of the belief itself'.[86]

In all these cases, the argument itself is not being attacked or promoted, because the arguer has gone straight to the source of the argument instead. In the example above, we don't even have a hint about what might make taxation a crime. This makes it a fallacy of irrelevance too.

You can see that this argument is closely related to the 'ad hominem' argument, where you attack the person instead of their argument. But the genetic fallacy gets a category of its own because the origin doesn't have to be a person – it can be the media, or religion, or any other number of wider institutions.

TRY IT OUT

Which two of the following arguments look like the genetic fallacy?

A. My parents told me the earth will crash into the sun by 2040, therefore it will.
B. My wife and I both have red hair so our children will have red hair as well.
C. I am not going to use a jerrycan to store fuel, because they were invented by the Nazis.
D. The Socialist party has long believed that the government should own the banks, but really banks should be owned by shareholders.

(Answer: A and C.)

POISONING THE WELL

Throughout history, attacking armies have destroyed village water sources by poisoning them with oil, rubble or other contaminants. Once the well is poisoned, the whole village is often unliveable. Similarly, defending armies in retreat have also poisoned wells so that attacking armies, once they take over the land, have nothing to drink. This happened recently – in 2014 and 2015, ISIS poisoned the wells in a number of Iraqi villages they attacked (as if burning down the houses, murdering the men and old women and selling the other women into slavery wasn't enough.)[87]

Medieval villagers in Europe put a new twist on this heinous act. They put around rumours that Jewish people were poisoning village wells. Thus, when a plague or disease (inevitably) erupted, the villagers blamed the Jewish people. Thus the idea of the rhetorical fallacy 'poisoning the well' was born.[88]

Poisoning the well in arguments involves pre-emptively attacking your opponent in such a way that when they attempt to argue back, they just confirm your original attack. This might sound tricky and abstract, but it has real world implications. For example, a state premier (let's call her Jane Bloggs) might say, 'The mainstream media are out to get me. Everything they report about me is a lie because they are dishonest and they hate me.' If you believe this, then anything that the media subsequently reports about Jane (that she kicks her dog or is involved in tax fraud, corruption and serial killings) just feeds into the narrative that the media is out to get her. The well is well and truly poisoned. If this view takes hold in a significant proportion of the population, nothing the media uncovers or reports will be believed, because it feeds into the 'out to get her' narrative. Paradoxically, it can strengthen Jane by making her look victimised rather than guilty. Like the genetic fallacy, it can be deranging.

This trick, although perfected into an epistemological crisis in recent times, has been around for millennia. It is a form of ad hominem (attacking the person) argument. Its particular insidiousness is that it 'gets in first' by attacking the other person and making their defences sound like proof of the original claim. For example, your workmate might say about your boss, 'Oh, he is very good at talking – he can spin a tale about how this year's sales figures are good. But when you look at what he is doing behind the scenes, that's another story.' So, what then happens when your boss competently reports that the sales figures this year are good? Instead of thinking 'That's good news', you think 'Am I just being taken in and duped by his smooth talking and slick-sounding arguments? I wonder what is happening behind closed doors?' Doing his job looks like evidence of your boss's shonkiness. The well was poisoned by your workmate in advance.

Philosopher Roberto Ruiz makes a good case that poisoning the well is linked to the other logical flaw of 'unfalsifiability'. (An unfalsifiable claim is one that can't be disproven.) Ruiz uses the example of the Salem witch trials.[89] Were certain women witches? Of course. What would happen if their sisters tried to defend them? Well, they were witches too. What happened if their husbands or their lawyers tried to defend them? Well, they were warlocks and in league with the devil as well. Off they all went to the flames, the prison or the local pond.

TRY IT OUT

Rate the following examples of poisoning the well from most to least effective in terms of persuading the average person.

- Before you listen to what Jane says about prisons, don't forget she was a criminal herself once, so how much can you trust her?
- The Vice Chancellor might present us with a university improvement plan, but she hasn't worked a day in academia in her life.
- Teachers have decided they hate me and they are just out to get me. It might only be day one of term, but I bet I'll have a detention by the end of the week.
- The honourable member opposite can talk under wet cement about plans, but let's see him actually implement one.

SPECIAL PLEADING

You see this fallacy everywhere, and particularly in traffic matters. People generally agree on road rules and etiquette – they line up in traffic, don't go through red lights, don't cut in. However, many people sometimes break these rules. Cutting in? 'I've had a rubbish day, and I just want to get home, so it's okay today if I drive up the left-hand lane and then merge back in.' Running a red light? 'I'm close to being late for this meeting, so it's okay just this once to drive through that amber light.' Going 8 kilometres per hour above the speed limit on a freeway? 'Hey, we're good people and we write nice books about critical thinking, so maybe we can get away with this.'

In effect, special pleading means you expect the rules to apply to other people but not so much to you. It is about thinking there is something special about you or your circumstances, apart from primary narcissism, that means you have a special get-out clause. Often it is unconscious. Sometimes it isn't.

We also can do it to benefit members of our family and friends. Bullying is bad and there should be zero tolerance of it in the playground. But if my son Harry is accused of bullying, it was just a bad day and the other child misinterpreted what Harry said, and it was probably just banter, and you should have seen what those older kids did to him last year and my son Harry is lovely around his younger cousins.

It doesn't just have to be about you or your family. It can be about how generous you are towards arguments or political sides you agree with and how much more critical you are of those on the opposite side. If a politician from the other side has been found pork barrelling, well, this is the sort of outrageous immoral behaviour you would expect from them. But if a favourite politician from your own side has gone against the rules to shower money on their local art gallery ... well, it's a good cause, and everyone is expected to go the extra mile for their own community and it must be tempting for anyone and no one's perfect. Special pleading is a form of double standard. It is also a form of cognitive dissonance: when someone you respect does something bad, you adjust your opinion of the act (was it really bad?) instead of the person (do I really respect them?).

Special pleading is part of our bias as humans. We are usually kinder to ourselves and our friends than our adversaries and enemies. However, when this leads to making special exceptions and excuses for yourself, and distorting reality so that your pristine opinion of your own view or correctness is maintained, you are engaging in special pleading.

TRY IT OUT

Review your behaviour. Can you think of times when you give yourself or your views a 'special pass' that you don't give to other people? If nothing comes to mind, think about:

- what you are like in traffic
- how you judge politicians on your own side of politics against those on the other side
- the day-to-day behaviour of your best friend (as opposed to someone you dislike)
- how you react to a referee's dodgy call in favour of your own team.

CHAPTER 6
THINKING FALLACIES OF PRESUMPTION

THE SLIPPERY SLOPE

The 'slippery slope' is a mixed blessing in the world of argument. When used badly it can persuade people of all sorts of exaggerated, unfounded and dreadful consequences, but when used properly it can be a sage caution against short-sighted decisions.

So, what is it? A 'slippery slope' is the claim that one act could lead to a series of other events that gather their own momentum and result, eventually, in a much bigger negative consequence. It is like a literal slippery slope – one step on the slope means you start to lose your footing and scramble to take another step, but you slip further down, and so on all the way to the bottom of the ravine.

A common example occurs in the gun debate. Some argue that if you use background checks to stop certified lunatics getting their hands on automatic weapons, there will be background checks on everyone and then all semi-automatic weapons will be banned and then all weapons will be banned and we will all be left cowering in fear of an imminent invasion by the microstate of Milesia. More domestically, this argument might be used to show your children that if they don't do their homework on Tuesday night there will be an inexorable set of events that lead to general academic failure, expulsion and becoming an unemployable, homeless wastrel on the streets.

Nonetheless, the slippery slope argument is often used more creditably. It is a regular feature in legal judgements explaining why a judge refuses to take an action. A colleague might ask to borrow some of your research to help them with a report for your joint manager. You say, 'Yes'. They then ask you to read their report. You say, 'Yes'. They then ask you to brainstorm the report one evening. You wearily say, 'Yes'. They then ask you to edit their report. You, through gritted teeth, say, 'Yes'. And so it goes until you might as well have written the report yourself. By failing to draw a line somewhere, you have engaged in slippery slope behaviour and let your colleague become a dependent time-drain on you. There was no one step – it was the slippery slope that ate up all your time.

The slippery slope is also known as 'the thin end of the wedge', 'the domino effect' and 'the floodgates effect'.

The proper use of a slippery slope argument can work to avoid corruption or moral dodginess. If you have a work expense card, it might not be too bad to get a cup of coffee on it (it helps keep you focused at work, after all), then maybe it is not so bad to get a few meals with it (hey, everyone eats on the job), then it might not be too bad to buy your partner a gift with it (after all, they put up with your long nights at the office), then maybe you could have a night away with your partner on it (maybe you will drive past a business opportunity on the way) and so on … all the way to the moment the company dime pays for your beautiful new house and the kids' school fees. Few people who commit fraud start with a million-dollar sting; they just bought that first cup of coffee.

The difference between good and bad slippery slope arguments is whether you can demonstrate the likelihood or plausibility of the steps in between. If you can show that each step would probably lead to the step after it, you have a good argument. On the other hand, if you can show a couple of points on the slope where you can 'dig your heels in' (as philosopher Nigel Warburton says[90]) or find a ledge, it is not a good argument. This is why people often talk about 'drawing a line' – it is the same thing as finding a ledge. For example, in the gun debate there is a big difference between restricting gun ownership for people who are unstable and preventing gun ownership for everyone. You can dig your heels in at the point where farmers need them, or where most people can have handguns, or where there are good background checks or waiting periods. There are plenty of clear points where you can draw a line if you want to.

TRY IT OUT

Which of these are good or appropriate uses of the slippery slope – and which aren't?

- We should ban alcohol. One drink leads to two drinks, leads to four drinks, leads to a lifetime of alcoholism.
- If I let you be 10 minutes late for work without saying anything, you will start thinking that's okay, then it will be 20 minutes and then half an hour.
- We should put a limit on gambling. You start with the poker machines saying you will just spend 20 bucks, but then you put $100 in, then $200, then you are pouring your whole week's salary into the machine.
- If we let children strike for the climate instead of going to school, the next thing you know they will be striking against racism, then striking for lower university fees, then striking for anything that takes their fancy that month.
- If we let AI write our essays for us, then it will be writing our thesis, then our government policy documents, then it might as well be doing all of humanity's work.

UNFALSIFIABILITY

An argument is unfalsifiable if it cannot be disproven. 'Hold on,' you might think, 'that can't be right. You mean an argument so excellent that nobody can find a good argument against it? That sounds like a *great* argument.' No, this is different. An unfalsifiable argument is one that by its very nature and structure is impossible to knock down. This doesn't make it stronger; it makes it weaker. It is the sheer impossibility of counterargument – its unfalsifiability – that makes it suspect. Admittedly this is a slightly mind-churning paradox. Let's show you how it works.

For example, have you ever wondered why sometimes your pens go missing? Why is it that you buy a pack of five pens and within a few weeks they are all gone? We have the answer for you. There is an army of little green goblins devoted to pen theft who take them back to their dark and inky grottos. They are cunning, scheming and clever. Seriously.

'What?' you ask. 'Have you ever seen one of them?'

'No, because they are invisible,' we reply.

'But I would have seen the pen being dragged along the table,' you say.

'No, no, no,' we reply. 'You've never seen a single pen being carried away because those goblins are experts at tracking your gaze and they make sure you are looking the other way before they do it. You have never seen any trace of them either? Well, that's just more evidence of how wily they are. They don't want to be caught, and they are damn good at it.'

... and that is an unfalsifiable argument. That it cannot be disproven makes it weaker not stronger.

You might think unfalsifiable arguments don't emerge in the real world, but they appear more often than you think. Twenty years ago, many countries went to war with Iraq because President Saddam Hussein was alleged to have weapons of mass destruction that he was about to unleash on the world. It turns out he didn't have any. The key UN agencies at the time made this clear: the UN chief weapons inspector Hans Blix testified that in their inspections they found nothing (although Hussein hampered their investigations). But finding no weapons was, for many people, insufficient evidence that there weren't any. Instead, it was evidence of how good Hussein was at hiding them. It showed again the wily deviousness of Hussein and why he needed to be overthrown. And so the invasion went ahead to strip Hussein of weapons he did not have. An unfalsifiable argument was used as a key plank of an invasion that almost everyone now admits was a mistake.

Unfalsifiability is the stock in trade of conspiracy theorists everywhere. Can't find evidence that UFOs have landed all over the world? That's because governments have hidden the wreckage of crashed ships in top secret military hangers. Can't find evidence that your local politician is running a slave trade and sex ring? That's how good they are at silencing and killing local officials. Can't find the scientific papers that prove the earth is flat? That is because of the vast conspiracy among those sphericist scientists who refuse to publish 'flat earth' papers in their elitist journals.

Unfalsifiable arguments can emerge in speculative sciences too. There is an argument in science that our whole universe is just one little speck in a multiverse. There are also arguments about what happened before the Big Bang, a cosmic explosion from which our universe emerged. Both these arguments, although beguiling, are unfalsifiable. We can't, and probably won't ever, detect these other universes (although some people are trying). We can't look back before the Big Bang to a realm without our familiar dimensions of space and time. So, beguiling as the argument that our universe is one atom in an amazingly vaster universe might be, it cannot be falsified and is much weaker as a result.

Unfalsifiability makes a statement fallacious but it does not make a claim wrong. Saddam Hussein might have been hiding weapons all along. Our universe might be an atom in a vastly bigger universe. There might even be goblins stealing your pens. It is just that unfalsifiability is very shaky ground on which to rely.

TRY IT OUT

Can you make up unfalsifiable arguments to justify the following claims?

- The government has bugged your house.
- Adolf Hitler fled to Argentina after World War II and spent 30 years living in hiding.
- A politician you don't like cheated in the last election.
- The world is actually balanced on a long line of invisible elephants standing on top of each other.

POST HOC ERGO PROPTER HOC

Jane joins a large trading company with a reputation as a very good trader. Within weeks the company's profits go up 10 per cent. Jane is a saviour, a hero. Her skills and expertise have clearly filled the coffers and boosted the bonuses of every trader in the company, right? Wrong (well, probably wrong). You will see the problem more clearly with a starker example. Jane goes for a walk around the block every morning at 5.00 am in the dark. Every morning, she says to herself, 'Sun come up, sun come up'. Within an hour or two every morning, the sun comes up! Jane is a saviour, a hero – her power and dedication have clearly caused the sun to get up off the horizon. Right?

Wrong.

In both cases, just because something came after something else, it doesn't mean it caused it. We have confused correlation with causation. The Latin term for this is 'post hoc ergo propter hoc' (after this, therefore because of this). In the case of Jane and the company, all sorts of things might have happened after Jane joined the company. Maybe the bond market went up, maybe they employed five other new great employees at the same time, maybe they kick-started a whizz-bang new computing system that month, maybe Jane's predecessor was a cheat who was defrauding the company ... or any of 25 other things.

We fall for 'post hoc ergo propter hoc' all the time. Jack joined a school in July and things started going missing from the changeroom in August, therefore Jack is a thief. I took a multivitamin tablet and felt great the next morning, so multivitamins work. I read this critical thinking book and won the lottery the next day, so critical thinking makes you rich.

This fallacy has a close sibling, 'cum hoc ergo propter hoc'. This means that because two things are connected (though one did not necessarily happen after the other) people think one thing caused the other. Often there is an underlying cause for both things. For example, on Tuesday morning two things happen in the city. Firstly, sales of takeaway coffee go up compared with the previous days. Secondly, a survey of 1000 people in the CBD shows they are much less happy than a survey of 1000 people in the CBD 48 hours earlier. Is caffeine a terrible depressant? No. Do people only drink coffee because they are unhappy? No. An underlying phenomenon is causing both – more people in the CBD are at work.

Author Ryan Holiday, who writes about Stoicism, points out that we make the same mistakes about people's character. We think people are successful because of their ego (and therefore we should have a big ego). But he points out famous people who are successful despite their ego, not because of it, such as basketballer Kyrie Irving. Holiday writes 'Kyrie Irving is not a great athlete because he has an ego. It's that his talent as a basketball player was great enough for three teams to absorb his ego in order to utilize those talents ... and even then this turned out to be a costlier bargain than they thought.'[91]

TRY IT OUT

Which of the following arguments look like post hoc ergo propter hoc, which are genuine causation and which are a bit murky?

- The rooster crowed. Then the sun came out. The rooster crowing caused the sun to come out.
- The sun came out. Then it got warmer. The sun coming out makes things warmer.
- I bought a Fitbit. Then I started exercising more. Buying a Fitbit made me exercise more.
- There were tax cuts. People started spending more. The economy improved. Tax cuts make the economy improve.
- My friend gave her lucky necklace to me. The next week she was in a fiery mid-air jumbo jet collision. Giving me the lucky necklace caused a fiery mid-air jumbo jet collision.

BEGGING THE QUESTION

Your partner, a fanboy of astrophysicist Neil deGrasse Tyson, says, 'Neil deGrasse Tyson is a great communicator.'

'Why is that?' you ask.

'Because he speaks so effectively,' your partner says.

But, you think to yourself, speaking effectively is basically the same thing as being a good communicator. The conclusion (great communicator) and the reason (speaks effectively) have merged. In fact, your partner hasn't really proved anything. The reasoning isn't exactly wrong – it's just that your partner hasn't given much of a reason at all. He may as well have just said, 'Neil deGrasse Tyson is a great communicator', then gone off to pour a glass of wine or have a nap.

This is 'begging the question', where someone states what they are trying to prove as one of the arguments for what they are trying to prove.

This lazy argumentation can get people to believe all sorts of things without actual evidence. 'The parliament can make these laws because it has the power of law making vested within it.' 'You should follow Bill because Bill is the leader' (this is also argument from authority). 'Everybody wants to eat at Papa's Pizza because it is the most popular pizzeria in town.'

Begging the question is one of the more frustrating fallacies – it is like a snake that eats its own tail so you cannot see where it begins and where it ends. Unsurprisingly, it also called 'circular reasoning'.

Begging the question has a long history. It comes from Aristotle, who called it 'asking for the initial thing'. It was called 'petitio principii' for centuries. Its most famous use historically is as a justification for a deity based solely on the existence of written religious texts. Let's contemplate the religion of the little green goblins (the ones who steal your pens). This religion can be understood by reading the divinely inspired book of *Goblinania*. You tell an acolyte of the little green goblins that you don't believe their religion and they tell you that its truth is all laid out in the book of *Goblinania*. 'But how do you know the book of *Goblinania* is true?' you ask. They might reply, 'Because every word of it is inspired by the Great Grinch of Green Goblins'. How do you know there is a Great Grinch of Goblins? Well, it's all there in the book of *Goblinania,* isn't it? And so on. It's a hall of argumentative mirrors that can do your head in.

Another form of begging the question is where the conclusion you want to prove creeps its way into the definition or description of what you want to prove. For example, you might say, 'Slimy and disgusting oil should be left in the ground.' But by defining oil as 'slimy and disgusting' you have already tried to make the case for why it should stay in the ground without needing to provide another reason. Other people might not find oil slimy and disgusting at all – they might find it useful and practical.

The use of the term 'begging the question' is changing before our eyes. People now also use it to mean 'begging *for* the question'. For example, someone might say, 'Little Johnnie is such a star footballer: he controls the ball beautifully, kicks precisely and can read the whole game in an instant. It begs the question why he hasn't been picked for the Under 8s side this year.' In this use of 'begs the question', the reasons force the question. 'Begging the question' used this way is a sign of overwhelming reasons, instead of no reasons at all.

TRY IT OUT

Rate the following 'begging the questions' from least to most extreme.

- I am in charge of this house because I am the parent.
- Dogs are the best companions because they love people the most.
- Vegetables are nutritious because they are packed with goodness.
- Everything I do is excellent because it says on this note I just wrote 'Everything I do is excellent'.
- The government should make these welfare decisions because it is the government.

SHIFTING THE GOALPOSTS/NO TRUE SCOTSMAN

The true Scotsman fallacy was first written about by English philosopher Antony Flew in 1971.[92] Flew imagined a Scotsman (let's call him Jamie) saying that no Scotsman puts sugar on his porridge.

Jamie's friend says, 'But I know Angus the Scotsman and he puts sugar on his porridge.'

Jamie replies, 'Ahh … but no *true* Scotsman puts sugar on his porridge.'

Our Scotsman made a strong generalisation – then a counterexample knocked it over. Rather than accepting defeat or moderating his statement, Jamie changed the definitions in the generalisation. By doing this he was making his argument unfalsifiable. The 'true Scotsman fallacy' is also known as the 'argument from purity'.

A solution to this problem is to include 'most', 'mainly' or even 'overwhelmingly'. If Jamie had said, 'Almost no Scotsman would do such a thing', he would have still been on strong ground, although he would probably have received a less rousing cheer from his friends at his rustic Scottish pub. But by cornering himself with an absolute statement he has created a problem.

There are examples of 'no true Scotsman' everywhere. Religions are held up by some as universally peaceful, so when someone points out counterexamples of a Christian person shooting up a mosque in Christchurch, an Islamic person flying a plane into a skyscraper in New York or a Hindu person letting off a bomb in Gujarat, the reply sometimes offered is 'But they are not true Christians/Muslims/Hindus'. What could be said more safely is that the overwhelming number of people in each religion are peaceful, that these murderers belonged to an extreme, fundamentalist wing of the religion, or that they were deranged loners.

There are many examples where excluding someone from a group would be okay because their acts put them outside the definition of the group no matter what they claim. If you went to dinner with a vegetarian and they ordered a T-bone steak, you would be within your rights to say, 'You are not a true vegetarian'. If someone claimed to be a Scotsman, but had lived in Thailand all his life, had 'pure' Thai blood extending back 20 generations and had never been to Scotland, you would be within your rights to say, 'You are not a true Scotsman'.

No true Scotsman is very closely linked to 'shifting the goalposts', where a definition, task or goal can be moved to thwart someone. Your boss might tell you you'll get a promotion if you get a postgraduate degree in business administration. You get the degree, but then your boss tells you that the promotions review board will focus only on increasing sales figures. The criteria changed – the goalposts shifted. This doesn't stop people from using multiple criteria when deciding promotions (for example, training, character and results) but when the focus changes unexpectedly, this is shifting the goalposts.

TRY IT OUT

Which are reasonable arguments and which are examples of 'no true Scotsman' or 'shifting the goalposts'?

A. Bob: You say you are a Christian, but in your house I only see images of Mohammed, Buddha, Shiva and Zeus. You go to the local Hindu temple to pray every day, and you never go to a church. I don't think you are a true Christian.

B. Freya: All Australians love sport.
Jane: I don't like sport – for me it is ballet all the way. And I was born and live in New South Wales.
Freya: Yeah, but all true Australians love sport.

C. Daughter: You said I could go out when I cleaned my room.
Mother: Yeah, but look at the mess you have made of the whole house. Really you need to clean the whole place up before you go out.

D. Phillipe: I didn't get the job?! You told me you would be looking at financial skills and I am the most qualified guy there is.
Mary: That is true. But we also needed to look at how any new employee would get on with their colleagues, and you are a narcissistic, boorish psychopath.

(A and D are reasonable arguments. B is 'no true Scotsman' and C is 'shifting the goalposts'.)

COMPLEX AND LOADED QUESTIONS

Imagine someone asks you, 'Have you stopped being awful to your best friend?'

'No,' you reply. What you mean is that you haven't been awful to your best friend at all. But what comes out with your 'no' is that you haven't stopped being awful to your best friend.

The problem is that there is no simple way to answer the question on its own terms without agreeing that you have been awful to your best friend one way or the other. A 'yes' answer means you used to be awful to your best friend. A 'no' answer means you are still being awful to your best friend.

This is because the question is a complex one with a hidden assumption in it: that you were, in the past, terrible to your best friend. Lots of questions have these hidden assumptions. 'Who is the king of Tonga?' has an assumption that Tonga has kings (in this case, it's reasonable as Tonga does indeed have a king). It is less reasonable when you ask, 'Who is the king of France?' The hidden assumption in the complex question becomes plainer (there hasn't been a king in France for more than 150 years).

People ask these questions in politics all the time. 'When is the prime minister going to come clean about what he knows about this scandal' assumes the prime minister is hiding something. 'Why did you treat me like rubbish at that dinner?' assumes you treated your partner or friend like rubbish at the dinner. Check for these assumptions in the questions you are asked.

TRY IT OUT

Can you make up a complex or loaded question about:

- climate change
- vote rigging at the local council election
- the beaches of Botswana
- cheating on your partner.

WEASEL WORDS

Few people like a weasel. They weasel around with their little weaselly bodies and forage their way into places they shouldn't go. They are famous for being able to suck the inside out of an egg, leaving just the empty shell for a bird to sit on in futile hope. This weaselly behaviour with eggs led to the sneaky concept of 'weasel words'.

Many people have been in companies that have been 'downsized' – or even worse, 'right-sized'. There has been employment 'realignment', people have been 'let go', often in order to 'pursue other interests'. These are all weasel words. They all mean people got sacked. In a company's defence, it would be difficult to write 'today we sacked 300 people'. But when saying something sensitively turns into oleaginous hiding from the real meaning, we have weasel words.

Weasel words are terms that are misleading or ambiguous, or that unduly hide the real meaning. They present in many ways – euphemisms and false authority, for example. Let's look at some members of this weaselly sub-species.

Euphemisms used deceptively are a form of weasel word that can be used to make something less unattractive than it really is. A war against another country might be called a 'regime change operation', a 'police action' or a 'proactive defence operation'. A clapped-out bomb of a car might be called 'pre-loved' by the salesperson in the car yard. When your child accuses a friend of not inviting them to her party, the 'friend' might reply, 'Oh, that wasn't a party, it was just a bunch of people who ended up coming to my house and hanging out and watching a video.' Okay, perhaps, if it was four friends – but pretty weaselly if it was 40.

Claiming **false authority** is another form of weasel words. Sometimes a news outlet will write 'critics love this movie' or 'researchers believe more wine leads to better health' or 'experts say more roads lead to longer journey times'. Which critics? Which researchers? Which experts? Without specifying, a speaker has just used false authority – another form of weasel words. A writer can use the phrase 'people are saying' to support a point without actually identifying those people.

The 'weasel words' concept might go even further and cut out people altogether. A company might say, 'We are regarded as the best car insurance firm in the business.' But by whom? Or to justify an evening drinking, you might say, 'It is believed that more wine leads to better health.' This use of the grammatical feature **passive voice** has let you off the hook: you haven't had to name any actual researchers, experts or pub-dwellers.

Advertisers use weasel words all the time. Some tricks include 'more' or 'less'. For example, a soft drink could have 'five per cent less sugar!!' Of course, this doesn't mean it has five per cent sugar – only that it has less sugar than some unmentioned product it is being compared with. If it has five per cent less sugar than the leading brand, which has 35 per cent sugar, it simply means it has 33.25 per cent sugar. It could also have five per cent less sugar than a bowl of sugar, which means it actually has 95 per cent sugar.

You will find weasel words all over the place, but now that you have a phrase for them, they will be easier to call out and put in their place.

TRY IT OUT

Rate the following weasel words from bad to worst.

A. Research indicates that wearing headphones affects your hearing.

B. Keith: Have you lost my AirPods?
Nicole: No, but I might have misplaced them long term.

C. Camilla: Are you asleep?
Charles: No, I am just resting my eyes.

D. James: Did you just sack me?
Rupert: I think it is easier to say we are giving you the freedom to find other opportunities.

E. Donald: Did you just invade that country?
Vladimir: No, we are conducting a national liberation operation.

F. It is proposed that we go to war with China.

G. Sales of our newspaper are up by five per cent.

FREE SPEECH AND CLICHÉS THAT END AN ARGUMENT

These linked fallacies are common in the wilds of social media. Someone makes a point that is objectionable, rude or demeaning. They are called out and criticised for it. Then they defend their previous statements by calling it 'free speech'. The fallacy is that they are free to say it, but that doesn't mean they are protected from criticism for saying it. People can go to town on someone else's views all they like without robbing them of their right to free speech. It is not censorship to tell someone you think they are wrong and objectionable. (Incidentally, you are not able to say absolutely anything you like. As the old law case says, 'You are not entitled to shout "fire" in a crowded theatre'.[93])

If Rapper Dud(z) sings that actress Marilyn M is a 'whiny blonde that should go back to the kitchen and the bedroom', Marilyn M might call him out as a misogynist jerk. It is no defence that he was merely exercising his right to free speech. His speech was free. No one was coming to arrest him. But he could be criticised for his view. People can feel they have been censored instead of criticised because the sting of criticism can be very personal.[94]

It is also worth considering the right to free speech versus the right to be heard. Just because someone's speech is free, other people are not obliged to listen to them. Great Uncle Alfred can go on all he likes about how solar panels give people cancer because they hold the melanomous rays of the sun, but people don't have to take him seriously. A thoughtful critical thinker might listen to a multiplicity of views, but they don't have to listen to everyone's views. If someone writes a physics paper that says Einstein's theories are wrong, and that gravity is a strange temporal field, they are free to write it, but no one is obliged to publish it and no one is obliged to read it.

This can go too far. 'Cancel culture' can broaden legitimate criticism of a statement or view to cover everything else that person said. It can also include attempts to cancel out that person's achievements or history.

'Argument-ending clichés' are associated with this. They stop an argument with a meaningless piece of folk wisdom that is hard to argue with. They do not relate to the substance of the argument or give the other person anything much to counter. For example, in an argument about the issues of competition someone might say, 'Well, it is what it is.' This cliché can halt the argument about competition in its tracks with a short shot of banality that adds nothing to the argument. Other examples of clichés that end arguments are 'Don't think so much about it' or 'It's all good' or 'Everyone has an opinion'. Just because it's catchy and sounds like your great-grandfather said it while building his log hut doesn't mean it's helpful.

TRY IT OUT

Try using 'free speech' or a cliché to end an argument about:

- climate change
- Josie's horrible behaviour to people in the office
- income inequality.

To help, here are a few handy clichés: 'People are people, what can you do?'; 'Fake news'; and 'Here we go again'.

SECTION III
REAL-TIME APPLICATION

CHAPTER 7

MAKING GOOD DECISIONS

Clear thinking is fundamental to making good decisions. Here, you'll find the elements of good thinking that should lead to better decisions and make a practical difference in your life. Applying the thinking in this chapter will increase the prospect of good decisions and will allow you to make decisions that are defendable, clear, balanced, sound and wise. Hopefully a good ROI for the next hour.

On a professional level the elements will help in large-scale decisions at work, either with colleagues or on your own. They will also assist with the smaller choices you make in your professional life several times a day, even if it simply means that you think for a few moments instead of jumping to an action or reaction.

They should also help with decisions in your personal life, from the biggest ones (such as buying a place to live), to less critical questions (such as where to go for dinner). They will help you come to a considered view about current affairs and issues in the public sphere. They might allow you to reflect more objectively on relationships with friends, family and colleagues. They might even help with the grocery shopping.

And even if you still don't get it quite right, you will know you made the best decision you could with the information you had at the time … even as you contemplate your circumscribed bank balance, useless mail-order exercise equipment or strained workplace relationship.

Overall, the process for making a good decision is not terribly difficult to step through and many business textbooks can give you apparently armour-plated procedures for good decisions. The devil can be in the detail, so this is what this chapter focuses on. One model, developed by the former intelligence agency analyst and founder of the *Farnam Street* blog Shane Parrish, is particularly thoughtful. In his book *Clear Thinking*[95] he describes the following steps:

Defining the problem: This is working out what issue you are trying to solve or what you are trying to achieve when making the decision.

Exploring possible solutions: This is coming up with a variety of different ways to solve your problem. It involves ways of overcoming your obstacles. This is often a creative, freethinking stage, but it also involves critical analysis.

Evaluate the options: Once you have a series of options in front of you, it is time to weigh them up and compare them with each other. This involves the most critical thinking and is the stage this chapter focuses on. Making decisions can also involve evaluating whether to make a change or stay the same, either of which can be reasonable options in different circumstances.

Do it: This means take the plunge and make the decision. You can be as smart, profound and multifaceted in your thinking as you like, but unless you are willing to act on your best assessments, you will not get anywhere. Making the decision can require some intellectual courage.

Learn from your decisions: Making the decision is not the end of the process. You can evaluate and reconsider based on what actually happens. Unexpected events will come your way, some of which you could have predicted and others you could not have.

EXPLORING POSSIBLE SOLUTIONS

This is the relatively free-flowing stage of finding a variety of different alternatives that might solve your problem or achieve your aim. The critical tools below will help with this stage, although it requires some strong creative thinking as well.

Considering the alternatives

When exploring possible solutions, you need to keep an open mind. This usually means you need to examine a few different alternatives. If you don't do this (or don't take the alternatives seriously) you have, in effect, made up your mind in advance; there was only *one* possible solution. This in turn does not give you much chance to think critically about your decisions. Everyone has been in this situation – the work meeting to 'discuss' something that was decided last week or the argument with your spouse about where to go on holiday when they are 'Hawaii or bust'.

Alec Fisher, the former Professor of Critical Thinking at the University of East Anglia,[96] points out that the alternatives for some decisions are straightforward, such as 'Will I have the beef or vegetarian lasagne?' Other alternatives require creative and imaginative solutions, such as 'How could we market our new line of vegetarian lasagne?'

Once you have your alternatives ready to go, you should ask yourself about the consequences of these alternatives. Should you sell your car and get public transport to work? The consequences of public transport might include the opportunity to read in the morning, the possibility of being sardined in the vestibule area, the greater likelihood of getting get wet and cold when it rains, and not having to find a park in the city. Consequences are a significant element in coming up with a rationale for a decision. Sometimes you will have to be creative or far thinking and it might be the most alert thinker in a room who comes up with the consequence other people didn't see. Decisions often come with unintended consequences. If you don't have a car and get public transport or a cab to your football games, you might end up regularly drinking too much at the post-match drinks. This might then cause a fallout with your partner. The recent coronavirus lockdowns came with a panoply of unintended consequences, from panic buying of toilet paper to the rapid acceptance of working from home by employers to stock shortages of jigsaw puzzles.

Fisher also suggests considering the likelihood of the future consequences as well as what the consequences might be. A significant consequence that is very unlikely to happen might or might not be about equal with a small consequence that is likely to happen. Entire risk industries have been created to systematise this balance into matrices and approaches. The legal world is also chock full of this approach. 'Reasonably foreseeable' risk is the subject of shelves of textbooks. If you are on the local council and decide to build a perfectly average swing set at the local park, is there a risk that someone will fall off it and graze their elbow? Yes, but the consequence is small so you could go ahead regardless. However, if you decide to put the new 'electro-zoomo-360-supersonic-swingo' in the local park without supervision, it's highly likely small children will fall off it and break their bones. It is unlikely you would go ahead with this highly foreseeable risk given its significant consequence. Between these extremes is a spectrum with different sets of risk and consequences.

It is important to distinguish between the reasonable risk of a consequence and the fanciful risk of a consequence. Fanciful means you can imagine the consequence, but it is extremely unlikely to happen. However, people mix up fanciful and reasonable risks all the time and don't do things they could have. This is because we can visualise in graphic detail a fanciful risk, which makes it feel more immediate. We are storytelling creatures, not statistical ones. With a normal set of swings, there is a fanciful risk that a kid could topple off it onto half-a-dozen thumb tacks the previous person had accidentally spilt on the ground from their earlier craft lesson, cut themselves open, be a haemophiliac and be rushed to hospital … all because of that swing you installed. But this is a fanciful risk only, and shouldn't stop you. Fear of air travel is a common example of people privileging the narrative of a risk happening (ie they can imagine the plane crashing) over the very low statistical chance of it actually occurring.

TRY IT OUT

Think through the alternatives and the foreseeable consequences for the following proposals:

- moving your child to a different school
- announcing to clients that your workplace is AI-free and all the work they receive will be done by humans
- introducing a set of guidelines for your child's social media use
- responding to a cyberhacker who has stolen your firm's data and is threatening to release it onto the web unless you pay a ransom within two hours
- making your employees come into the workplace more frequently.

Using criteria

Criteria can siphon an ocean of mental impressions, reasons, contradictions and feelings into a much calmer series of mental rivers to navigate as you explore different possible solutions. Using criteria is a good thinking tool because they often are organisational categories of reasons that can be used to make a decision or judgement.

Take house hunting for example. You see six places in a day. One place has an extra bedroom, another place is close to the bus, a third is on the top floor, a fourth is brand new, a fifth has a bit of a garden, a sixth is much too expensive. You come home exhausted and confused. This goes on week after week, month after month. You lose out at a few auctions and become more and more overwhelmed with each new set of properties. Eventually you buy something because you generally like it, because you can semi-afford it, and because otherwise you are in danger of abusing the next real estate agent who tells you the cupboard you walked into is actually the third bedroom.

This is not a great way to make what is probably the largest financial commitment of your life.

Establishing a set of criteria of what matters to you in advance helps you sort through, explore and negotiate the many impressions in your head. For example, you could use the criteria:

- proximity to transport
- size of bedrooms
- parking space
- modern building
- location on a main or secondary road
- price.

You can even give each one a point score so each place you look ends up with a total score. Then, when you walk into apartment 23, you can immediately see it through lenses that feel more considered, rational and calm. The price you are willing to pay for something will then depend on how it stacks up against your pre-established criteria.

In a meeting, merely invoking criteria can transform the gathering from a generalised talkfest into a constructive, ordered discussion. It makes the implicit basis for a decision explicit. You can use explicit criteria as a sort of operating system in your brain to decide which firm to work for, which school to send your kids to, which university to go to, which new computer system to implement at work. But don't go overboard. If you begin using criteria to work out whether to get the pavlova or the tiramisu for dessert, you might find yourself falling off dinner invitation lists.

A criterion is different from a rule. A rule is a definitive statement telling us what to do, such as 'Drive at 60 kilometres per hour'. Criteria, in contrast, form the basis for a judgement. We might have criteria for what makes a good driver, but we don't have criteria for whether you drove over 60 kilometres per hour. Either you did or you didn't.

Sometimes criteria and rules can blur. For example, the statement 'Check the grammar of your submission before you send it on' can be a criterion for good writing or a simple rule you should follow.

Other frequently used terms are simply criteria dressed up. 'Standards for evidence', 'aims of organisations' and 'exclusion policies' are all other ways of imposing criteria. Used properly, criteria can also be standards others will hold you to. If you make it clear that you are going to employ someone based on their qualifications, experience, drive and ability to work with people, and you employ the unqualified, inexperienced, lethargic, rude son of the CEO, unsuccessful applicants may well have a case against you.

Explicitly using criteria can be a key tool for coming to rational decisions in many areas of your life. They force you to make overt the standards or reasons you are using to make comparisons or judgements. They can transform a morass of data and perceptions into an ordered set of factors for your decision.

TRY IT OUT

Come up with a set of criteria for the following decisions:

- what car to buy
- whether to go to war with another nation
- which book to give a literary prize to
- whether to invest in software startup X or software startup Y
- what job to take
- where to go on holiday.

EVALUATING YOUR OPTIONS

This is the stage where you weigh up, compare and assess the options. The tools below will help you evaluate the options.

Necessary and sufficient conditions

Let's imagine that Sven wants to start a new basketball team for the local competition. Sven is a good coach, and a lot of people want to join the team. Potential players have to answer questions on a form to get a tryout. The first question on Sven's extensive form is 'Are you legally blind?' We could call Sven picky, but he expects everyone on his basketball team to be able to see. For Sven, this criterion is a 'necessary condition'. If you are unable to see, it doesn't matter what else you've got – great height, good attitude, an orange farm for an endless supply of oranges at half time – you don't get a tryout. Sight is a necessary condition for Sven's team.

Other questions cover elements Sven might like. Where did you play basketball before? Do you have your own transport? Do you like drinking beer after the game? His last question is 'Were you the captain of your competition-winning team at school?' Sven has decided that everyone who captained their competition-winning team at school gets a tryout. It doesn't matter how many of these people turn up, he is going to give them all a run. This criterion is a 'sufficient condition' to get a tryout. It doesn't matter if they are short, have a bad attitude, do not own an orange farm, do not have their own transport and hate beer – they will still get a tryout. Captaincy of a competition-winning team is sufficient.

In short, a necessary condition (eg sight in a basketball team) is one that is essential for an outcome to occur.

A sufficient condition (eg having captained a successful school basketball team) is one that is a guarantee for an outcome to occur.

Necessary and sufficient conditions can also help you make logical leaps. If you can't be elected to parliament unless you are an Australian citizen and you meet someone who is in parliament, you can assume they are an Australian citizen because it is a necessary condition.

Establishing necessary and sufficient conditions can be instructive in evaluating different options. In the example of house hunting, if a parking space is a necessary condition, any unit without a carpark is immediately excluded. If you walk into a unit without a carpark, you can walk straight back out again, even if it turns out to be a palatial harbourside mansion with 270-degree views and a bonus tiger cub in the jacuzzi. On the other hand, a sufficient condition is one where as soon as it is achieved, all the other criteria melt away. For example, a 270-degree harbour view might be a sufficient condition for you. It doesn't matter what sort of dump it is, or how tiny, termite infested or compromised by the unmistakable signs of a poltergeist it is; if it has a 270-degree harbour view you will jump at it.

When looking for a job, a necessary condition might be a salary of $50,000 a year (without it, you don't care if the job will eradicate disease and save the world) and a sufficient condition might be a salary of $50,000,000 per year (as long as they pay you this much, you don't care if the job involves spreading disease and ruining the world). When looking to interview a field of potential employees, it might be a necessary condition that they have a relevant degree and a sufficient condition that they currently doing the same job in a similar company. Working out necessary and sufficient conditions allows you to evaluate and clarify what factors in your criteria are the most important.

TRY IT OUT

Which of the following are closer to necessary conditions and which are closer to sufficient conditions? Which are neither?

- You are employing a new architect for your firm.
  - They have an architecture degree.
  - They have won a major an architecture award.
  - They have a bright disposition at the interview and are personable.
- You decide to send your child to a new school.
  - It has good academic results.
  - Lessons are in person, not online.
- You are going to vote for a local member.
  - They are not a serial killer.
  - They agree with you on all your views.
- You are deciding about your overseas holiday.
  - It has brilliant and very cheap accommodation where you are pampered every moment of the day.
  - You can get there by plane.

Being consistent (most of the time)

When attempting to evaluate options for a course of action, it is superficially attractive to cherry-pick arguments that look or sound good, regardless of how those various arguments fit together – or even if they don't. This is particularly the case when you source your arguments from multiple places.

For a decision (or an argument) to be strong, however, the reasons for it should be consistent with each other. This means all the justifications should be true at the same time. Without this consistency, an opponent of the decision can easily dismantle it. If the arguments are inconsistent, it often means that the decision or overall argument is not sound.

For example, vocal and time-rich members of the local football club the Leopards might decide to take a proposal for a new leopard-skin sunhat for spectators to the board. This, members say, is a battle of principle to see whether the board really cares about their club. Their reasons are: firstly, the sunhats are needed to build morale among the spectators; secondly, the board has already approved a leopard-skin football shirt, trousers, scarf and socks, so there is precedent for leopard-skin clothes; thirdly, it would show that the board really does encourage the enthusiasm of the spectators; and finally, the hats are needed so fans can be clearly identified at the game and on public transport.

However, the second argument here blows a hole through the other arguments. If fans of the Leopards already have leopard-skin shirts, trousers and scarves, why do they need a hat for morale? Why haven't these other items of clothing already created the hoped-for esprit-de-corps? The same inconsistency applies to identification on public transport and at the game: if you can't be identified by your leopard-skin shirt and trousers, then people are not suddenly going to notice your hat. The argument about precedent, while perfectly sound on its own, undercuts the other arguments. Perhaps the members should consider whether fans really want to be seen wearing leopard skin at all.

These sorts of inconsistencies might creep into our overall world views and opinions too. Some people might claim at one and the same time that 'morals are all relative' and 'slavery is wrong everywhere and in both the present and the past'. It is hard to hold these two arguments together. Part of the issue here is that both statements are phrased as absolutes – *all* morals are relative, and slavery is wrong *everywhere* and at *all times*.

It is useful to remember that there are several types of consistency. Firstly, there is logical consistency, which we have already looked at. There is also practical consistency. This is where your statements don't line up with how you act. If you say that you are a 'family man/woman' but spend 16 hours a day at work, you are not being practically consistent.

Inconsistency isn't always a bad thing. If an Airbnb property has mainly five-star ratings for cleanliness, but quite a few people have given the place only three stars, you might be slightly on your guard and think the cleaning service is patchy (though it might just mean some people are pickier than others). The apparent inconsistency gives you good information. Sometimes apparent consistency can be suspect and prompt you to ask more questions. After all, 99.01 per cent of people in Germany in 1938 voted for the Nazi Party. (Really? It is perhaps worth asking whether the lack of other political parties and general terror were contributing factors.)

A few more cautions. Just because arguments are consistent it doesn't mean they are true. We might think the sun goes around the Earth because we see it rise in the morning, it looks smaller than the Earth, we see it go down every night and we see other objects going around the Earth at night, like the stars. This is all consistent, but it is not correct.

And just to make things a little more complex, the need for consistency in decision-making needs to be balanced with 'both/and' thinking (coming up).

TRY IT OUT

Spot (and explain) the inconsistent arguments in the following:

- I would make an excellent employee because:
    - I drive the team hard.
    - I will attend to staff welfare.
    - I take no prisoners.
    - Results are what matters to me.
- We, the Government, should subsidise mining coal because:
    - We need a reliable power source for the next decade.
    - There are thousands of jobs at stake.
    - Other forms of power have now become cheaper and more dependable – coal can't compete.
    - It looks better in the environment than windmills all over the hills or solar panels on every roof.
- Come to school X:
    - We have a place for everyone.
    - We love all-rounders.
    - We have an unremitting focus on academic success.
    - Find your own passion here.
    - We care about what matters to everyone individually.

Going from 'either/or' to 'both/and' thinking

'Either/or' thinking serves us better than 'both/and' thinking when we have simple decisions to make: 'Shall I order the beef or chicken for dinner?'; 'Shall I go to Spain or Mexico for my holiday?'; 'Do I marry Tom or Ryan?' (Both/and thinking might in fact be quite calamitous in this last example.)

However, as problems become more multifaceted, either/or thinking can close down thinking or prompt us to come up with simplistic solutions: 'Does my company pursue short-term profits or long-term sustainability goals?'; 'Should I spend my company's money on marketing or research and development?'; 'Should we focus on our mortgage or go on a holiday?' Either/or thinking can also be seen as 'binary thinking', or a red/green flashing light in our head that makes us choose one path over another. This is why both/and thinking is particularly important when evaluating the options to make a decision.

Several deep parts of our nature tend us towards the either/or solution. It is cleaner and less complex to deliver. It is more understandable to outside people. It can make you look more decisive and not given to compromise.

This doesn't just happen in our personal and work lives – it happens in our politics too. There are relatively few independent voters in many parts of the world and many people stick with a dichotomous Labor/Liberal, Republican/Democrat-type allegiance so strongly that good ideas from the other side or creative compromises don't get considered seriously … or at all. Many will dismiss science, statistics and facts offered by others if they disagree with their political outlook.

This is linked to the concept of 'paradox'. A paradox is when two contradictory phenomena can somehow be true at the same time (for example, 'You can't get a job without experience, but you can't get experience without a job'). Paradoxes can be very discomforting to the clear-minded thinker. However, as F. Scott Fitzgerald said in his 1936 essay 'The Crack Up', 'the test of a first-rate intelligence is the ability to hold two opposed ideas in mind at the same time and still retain the ability to function'.[97]

This is not just saying, 'Should I eat chicken or beef for dinner … great, I'll have both!' It is about setting up different possibilities for more complicated solutions. A company that decides to focus on marketing in the short term and research and development for future projects has myriad ways to do this.

In her 2016 *Harvard Business Review* article 'Both/And Leadership' Wendy Smith called this 'consistent inconsistency'.[98] While it is well-intentioned for people to be consistent, she wrote, it doesn't work for senior people in an organisation who have to go into the job appreciating multiple truths that often conflict with each other. Instead, they need to accept the cognitive dissonance that comes from managing the different stakeholders, focuses and elements of a big organisation. Either/or is too simple for this, she says.

Various traditional adages tell you not to take the both/and route when evaluating options. They include 'Don't be neither fish nor fowl' and 'Nail your colours to the mast'. Sometimes this is true. Done poorly, a both/and solution just leads to a compromise where no one is happy (or, in the case of 'Shall we pay off our mortgage or go on a holiday or buy that jewellery or eat out every night', you go broke). However, a resolutely either/or attitude can just look for clear and decisive action at the expense of more considered and creative solutions. Both/and solutions are very often more effective.

TRY IT OUT

Can you think up potential both/and solutions for these dilemmas? Sometimes this will also involve identifying the either/or extremes.

- the issue of young people and drug dependencies
- eating meat during a climate emergency
- beautiful Persian rugs are often made with child labour
- countries have very differing taxation rates, leading companies to base themselves in countries with very low taxation rates
- I want to climb mountains for my holidays and my partner wants to shop in cities.

Drawing distinctions

Drawing distinctions involves taking two incidents, events or phenomena that are similar and pointing out what is different about them. It can be an important part of evaluating different options for a decision, and it is a key part of argumentation too.

For example, you might have a sushi franchise that has worked brilliantly in the suburbs around you. Under your business model, you build on main roads and near railway stations and get a lot of passing traffic. You look at a map of your city and think, 'Great, let's build a half-a-dozen more.' You select another five sites. But you should spend time drawing distinctions between the successful sites and the sites you have chosen, or you might end up with a string of sushi flops. The main road on one site might be a freeway – no one would stop or walk in. This distinction would make all the difference in the world. Another suburb might have an ethnic population that generally doesn't eat sushi. You could try being the trailblazer who convinces them, but it might be a very hard sell. A third suburb is in a demographic that often can't afford sushi. A fourth might have four already established sushi bars and be a saturated market. And so on. After the success of your first three shops, you could open another five shops that all fail because you didn't draw distinctions between the sites.

Drawing distinctions based on the facts often reduces injustice as well. It is a well-known procedure in legal circles to avoid precedents by making distinctions based on the facts. A school principal might expel one child for threatening a teacher and throwing a chair out the window but merely send another to counselling for doing almost exactly the same thing. This might look inconsistent. Certainly, the parents of the child who was expelled would probably make that point forcefully. However, one child might have been provoked by the teacher who called him a complete loser, while the other child might have threatened a teacher who had given their heart and soul to help them. One child might be an A-grade student with a perfect record whose father walked out of his marriage the night before, while the other child might have been warned for throwing furniture twice already. One class might have been a Drama improvisation lesson in which students had been passing chairs to each other, and the other might have been a third-floor Maths class and it was the teacher's chair that had sailed out the window onto the crowded courtyard below. Moving away from rigid consistency and insistence on precedence, and analysing what could be different about each situation, can lead to better justice.

It is also helpful to think about 'differences in degree' and 'differences in kind' when evaluating different options. A difference in degree highlights the difference between two things that are similar or of the same type. It is often usually just a difference in magnitude. In contrast, a difference in kind is a comparison where the differences are much more fundamental. They are a difference in category or type.

For example, you might be deciding on a pet for your family. The difference between a Cavoodle, a Pomeranian or a Highland Terrier would be a difference in degree. They are different in terms of size, nature and capacity to wander free in the highlands, but they are all small dogs. The differences are in magnitude of things in the same category or type. In contrast, choosing between a cat, a dog and a leopard is a difference in kind. It is a more fundamental distinction that will impact how often you take your pet for a walk, how much love and affection you get from your pet, and your chances of dying a violent and horrible death in front of your family in the coming months.

Analysing whether something has a difference in kind can also help separate situations that appear superficially similar. Shooting someone on a suburban street versus shooting someone in a war is a distinction in kind, not degree, even if the act is practically identical. So is smoking marijuana for recreation versus smoking it for pain relief during invasive cancer treatment.

Whether something is a difference in degree or kind is often a shifting carpet. It can depend on the purpose of the question. When asking, 'Should I buy a unit or shares as investments?', the difference between one unit and another down the street is small – a difference in degree. When asking, 'Which unit in this street should I buy as an investment?', the difference between one unit and the unit down the street is critically large. It is the whole choice.

Some distinctions aren't really distinctions at all – they are just there to fool you. These are known as 'false distinctions' or 'distinctions without a difference'. Next time your football coach yells at you, 'I don't want you try to kick that ball into the goal; I want you to *actually kick* that ball into the goal' you can say they have made a false distinction because how do you intentionally kick a ball into a goal without trying? This is also a good way to get yourself dropped from the team the next week.

TRY IT OUT

What are the distinctions between the following items? Are they distinctions in degree or distinctions in kind? To answer this, you may have to decide why you are making the distinction.

- peas and cauliflower
- a cow and a human being
- choosing NRMA insurance or GIO insurance
- choosing to work for NRMA or GIO
- a six-week-old foetus and an 18-week-old foetus
- the richest person in Australia and the poorest person in Australia
- going 20 kilometres per hour over the speed limit to get your partner to the hospital to have a baby and going 20 kilometres per hour over the limit to get your partner to the hospital to visit her sister who had a baby
- the prime minister and the opposition leader
- attending a government school or attending a Catholic school.

Using hypotheticals

Hypotheticals are a great way to stress test different options. They allow you test rules. They also allow you to flush out the borderline cases that turn so many black and white decisions into shades of grey.

The military uses hypotheticals all the time to help them make decisions. What would happen if the enemy came over that mountain, or pre-emptively attacked our navy, or fried our technology in a cyberattack? This is what wargaming is about. A company looking to set up a chain of boutique coffee shops could run hypotheticals about other companies opening coffee shops or franchising. Modelling is also a form of hypothetical. Hypotheticals allow you to explore consequences and uncover prejudices. They get the imagination going too: Hypothetically, what would happen to society on earth if we raced to colonise Mars in the next 20 years, or what would happen to our social bonds if the climate increased by five degrees in the next century? Imagine you woke up as the president of your major business rival. How would you try to beat your own company?

TRY IT OUT

How do these hypothetical situations help you consider the issues around them?

- Interest rates rise to more than 10 per cent.
- Transporting goods becomes automated.
- Artificial intelligence becomes conscious.
- You go to the UK for your holiday and the trains go on strike.
- You are standing on a railway overpass. A train is coming down the track. You can see it is about to knock over and kill five maintenance workers standing on the track. If you pull a lever to change the points, the train will instead go down another track and kill a man who is standing there eating his lunch (this is called the 'trolley dilemma').
- Nobody stands in queues.

DO IT

After evaluating your different options, the time for action comes. You need to make the decision. What we have focused on here includes how to make decisions 'on the balance' and how to prioritise decisions.

Making 60-40 decisions

Much as we might wish otherwise, making decisions clearly is not formulaic. You cannot input an issue into one side, send it through the processes of 'considering the alternatives', 'using criteria' etc, and have a well-formed, ethical, strategic and tactical set of decisions emerge in a guaranteed way at the other end. If we could, everybody would make the right decisions all the time.

Nonetheless, this is what much of society expects. It is particularly true of government and politics. There is little room for equivocation when a government is selling a policy such as reducing the company tax rate by five per cent. The government might thunder about saving corporations from the yoke of excessive taxation as if the health of the capitalist system depended on it. The opposition might say it is just more evidence that the government has forgotten the everyday worker and taxpayer. The debate will probably be passionate, an all or nothing affair. The daily oppositional drip feed of this approach perpetuates the erroneous idea that decisions that matter are either entirely right or entirely wrong.

Instead, when you make a decision, it is often prudent to accept that it is 'on balance'. Think of it as a 70-30 or 60-40 decision. This can also make it easier to make the decision in the first place. It's not necessarily some failure of yours that you didn't get to the 100 per cent solution or see perfectly into the future. It can also positively affect how you explain or sell the decision to others. If you can say, 'There were good points either way, but ultimately we have decided to go in this direction', the people who were on the other side don't feel as sidelined, ignored or defeated. They are more likely to shrug and think, 'Well, I don't agree, but I can see why they decided this'.

This is particularly true when you have competing right decisions. A simple competing right decision is whether it would be better to take the great job you have been offered with one hospital or the great job you have been offered with another hospital. They are both great jobs, so extra angst spent making the 'perfect' decision is time wasted.

More insidious are competing wrong decisions, or least worst options. They happen when it is easy to see the downsides of every option (and are exacerbated by the whole army of people who tell you what's wrong with any option without having to make the decision themselves). Is it worse to get a crowded and unpleasant train to work or sit in a traffic jam for an hour and a half? Whatever you decide, if you have a crummy time getting to work you didn't make a bad decision – there just wasn't a magical, helicopter-shaped, good decision to make. If you are an impoverished, coal-producing, equatorial African nation, should you stop mining coal? If you are an education minister who needs to make cuts across the board after the prime minister decides to trim five per cent out of every department budget, do you cut into building classrooms, teacher salaries, teacher training or something else?

This is not an excuse for sloppy preparation or a failure to gather evidence. If your partner has booked a trip to Nepal in the middle of the monsoon period when it always rains and the paths get washed away, they can't really call 'foul'. If you install your drive-through coffee shop on a road with no traffic (or on the site of three previous failed drive-through coffee shops) then you have been negligent. But decisions made sensibly and in good faith should be able to withstand some censure.

Knowledge of 60-40 decisions is also not an excuse for dithering or endless delay. If you don't buy property because every open for inspection reveals at least one reason why you shouldn't, the net result is that you never own a property. Failing to make a decision is a decision in itself.

So, after doing your due diligence and gathering reasons for decisions, go ahead and make them. But don't treat that decision as the only possible right answer. Explain to yourself and others both the reasons for and the reasons against a decision and why you went the way you did. Don't let the perfect decision be the enemy of the good decision.

TRY IT OUT

What would a 60-40 decision look like in some of the following areas? What are the 60 per cent reasons and the 40 per cent reasons?

- You are a liver transplant doctor. One liver comes in. You have two compatible people in the hospital on the waitlist, a 35-year-old woman with three small children who has a job at Woolworths and an unmarried woman without children who is doing valuable research into cancer as part of a team at the University of Sydney. The person who does not get the liver will die. Who do you give the liver to?
- You consider voting differently at the next election.

- You rent a property in the CBD for your 40-employee wealth management firm. Rents are expensive, but you are managing. Only 10 employees on average come into the city to work even though there are 40 desks. You would like more people to come in. There are plans among the employees who come in to work to attract more of their colleagues each day. Your landlord suddenly puts another part of the building with eight spaces instead of 40 on the market at less than a quarter of your current rent. Your landlord will not negotiate on cutting back on your current leasehold – you have to take the 40-person site or the eight-person site. If you take the eight-person site, employees will have to hot desk. There are no other properties for lease in the CBD. Do you stick with the 40-person property or take the eight-person property?
- You are a school principal. Chris, who has been suspended twice and is on his last warning, has assaulted another student, Jade, who muttered something racist at him. Chris has been doing much better academically in the last six months and has been working shifts at Coles since his parents' marriage broke up six months ago. Chris begs you not to expel him because he is just turning his life around despite all the bad stuff around him. Jade says the racist comment she muttered was just a joke and that she is now very scared of Chris. Do you expel Chris?

Prioritising (it's more than a list)

Prioritising is a meta activity (it involves deciding about deciding). Once you have decided to do a series of tasks, you have to work out what to do when. This is the bread and butter of work, but it's crucial to be deliberative about it. Prioritising your decisions and activities can be almost as important as making them in the first place. Of course, prioritising is also important for day-to-day tasks that don't require much thinking. Wash the dishes, do the laundry, walk the dog or binge Netflix? That still needs prioritising.

Some people juggle prioritisation effortlessly in their head. We very much admire them, but most people deal with the work by creating a list on a scrap of paper. While this can be helpful, it has its limitations. What happens when the list has 47 things on it and the clock is ticking? You can mark a third of them with a big red 'U' for urgent, but that's still fairly cumbersome. Here are two options.

Urgent versus important. Perhaps a great number of urgent tasks land on your desk every day. A fusillade of emails need something done by yesterday, there are runaround activities and endless meetings about the latest operational glitch. Then there are things that are clearly important – advancing the strategic plan, finishing a major work, spending time with your parents or children. You know they are important, but they can get lost in the shrieking chorus of the day-to-day.

Some tasks are both urgent and important (for example, keeping the rods in the nuclear reactor cooled). Some are neither (for example, Bob from marketing has polled everyone to see whether he looks better in a blue suit or a grey suit). Some can be one or another. Putting tasks in a table instead of a list might help:

	URGENT	NOT URGENT
IMPORTANT	**Urgent and important**	**Important but not urgent**
NOT IMPORTANT	**Urgent but not important**	**Not important not urgent**

This table was used by President Eisenhower and popularised by Stephen Covey in *The 7 Habits of Highly Effective People.*[99] Eisenhower's model comes with helpful tips such as 'delegate' for 'urgent but not important' and 'eliminate' for 'not important, not urgent', which is fine for a president, but less of an option for most of us.

The most interesting quadrant is the top right one – important but not urgent. This is where the strategic, long-range, most fundamental work is often done. Without that quadrant flashing orange at you, it is possible to lose important, long-range tasks altogether. This very book is a good example of the top right quadrant for us. We both have jobs, careers and families we love. Not a single word of the drafts of this book was urgent. It was written early in the morning and late at night over quite a few years and on a sabbatical. But it was always important to us, because critical thinking is. So, little by little, the book was written. Without that top right quadrant, it never would have got past the 'Hey, wouldn't it be a good idea if …' stage.

Hopefully you can see the ease with which these quadrants allow you to prioritise, plan, manage, focus and limit your tasks. It is a list with muscle, which can make you much more effective at implementing decisions and doing tasks.

The Gantt chart. The Gantt chart was 'invented' by Henry Gantt in the US between 1910 and 1915 although there is plenty of evidence of them before that. They have been used to organise war efforts, build projects and even implemented in Soviet five-year plans. They have become much more popular in the past few decades.

The beauty of a Gantt chart is that you see every job at once. You can see when they start and how long each one will take. You can see who does them and which ones rely on others. They can be adapted for almost anything.

PROJECT TASKS	Jan	Feb	Mar	Apr	May	Jun	Jul	Aug	Sep	Oct	Nov	Dec
Task 1: Research	x	x										
Task 2: Planning		x	x									
Task 3: Development			x	x	x							
Task 4: Testing				x	x	x						
Task 5: Deployment					x							
Task 6: Review						x	x					
Task 7: Feedback analysis							x	x				
Task 8: Improvement								x	x			
Task 9: Final testing									x	x		
Task 10: Launch										x	x	

Once you have a set of tasks, spreading them across a second dimension allows you to maintain, manage and juggle them. By looking down the chart on a particular day you can quickly see what's complete and what's outstanding.

Once you have a decision, implementing it is important. A Gantt chart and an importance/urgency quadrant will help you prioritise, shuffle and get things done.

TRY IT OUT

- Make a Gantt chart for an activity you need to do.
- Make a Gantt chart for the hours in a Saturday, just to sample it.
- Make a 'to do' list, then transfer each of its tasks into the four important/urgent quadrants. How many are in each quadrant? What did this make you reflect on in terms of dividing or prioritising your time?

LEARN FROM YOUR DECISIONS

The decision and its implementation is not the end of the process. Part of decision making is going back and reviewing it. Occasionally there is the opportunity to unmake a decision that has not worked out. More often, looking over the decision again buttresses you for next time.

Unknown unknowns and 'black swan' thinking

The striking concept of 'unknown unknowns' has been around since the 1950s, but it was made famous (or perhaps infamous) by Donald Rumsfeld, the US Secretary of Defense in 2002, when he tried to explain why no weapons of mass destruction had been found after invading Iraq. He asserted:

> *Reports that say that something hasn't happened are always interesting to me, because as we know, there are known knowns; there are things we know we know. We also know there are known unknowns; that is to say, we know there are some things we do not know. But there are also unknown unknowns – the ones we don't know we don't know. And if one looks throughout the history of our country and other free countries, it is the latter category that tend to be the difficult ones.*[100]

Rumsfeld was widely criticised for this at the time. (It didn't help that there were no weapons of mass destruction in Iraq.) However, the concept he was explaining is sound.

Unknown unknowns are part of a quadrant of elements that we do and don't know when trying to make or review a decision. We will focus here on making a decision to make the unknown unknowns clearer, but usually you apply this to decisions that have already been made.

Known knowns	Known unknowns
Things we both were aware of and understood well.	Things we could predict or anticipate, but we didn't know if they were going to happen, or we didn't really understand them.
Unknown knowns	**Unknown unknowns**
Things we were not aware of, but the knowledge was out there (maybe someone else knew it).	We had no idea what they were, so we couldn't understand or plan for them.

Let's look at some examples to make decisions about a more prosaic issue: your next holiday to Greece.

Known knowns: The price of your airline ticket, the dates you are away, where Athens is, the bus timetable, etc. These are elements you can rely on when planning.

Unknown knowns: The best hotel in the town of Napflio or the best tour guide to take you to Delphi, etc. You don't know this information yet but people on the ground will. You could try a variety of travellers' sites, but when you get there, you'll be able to unearth some local knowledge. More investigation can bring unknown knowns up into the known knowns category.

Known unknowns: Whether the ferries that travel to the islands will be cancelled if you travel there in winter. You wouldn't know whether it was going to happen, but it was a risk you knew about. Other things in this category could include currency fluctuations, extreme weather events, kids getting sick – factors you can't know but you can imagine.

(If you work in risk mitigation, you spend most of your time working in this quadrant.)

Unknown unknowns: We can't give you examples of these for a Greece holiday. If we could, they would immediately become known unknowns and would move to that quadrant instead. So, we know they might occur during the holiday in theory but can't specify any. That's why unknown unknowns are so unnerving – as soon as you identify them, they turn into something else, but you know they are always out there somewhere (cue eerie music).

There are some spectacular corporate examples of unknown unknowns. How could typewriter manufacturers in the 1970s have predicted the computer revolution and the disappearance of their whole industry within a decade? Could companies with a stake in film technology making decisions in the 1980s have predicted the digital photography that wiped out their industry? Could horse breeders planning their new horse stud in the late nineteenth century have predicted the motor vehicle?

Unknown unknowns exist in the realm of psychology as well as corporate business. Psychologists Joseph Luft and Harrington Ingham introduced the phrase 'unknown unknowns' to their field of study. They created a construct called the 'Johari Window'[101] (a combination of their first names), which stressed personal development. We have created one here for a fictional worker.

	Known to self	**Not known to self**
Known to others	Friendly Capable Hardworking	Indecisive Can give confusing explanations
Not known to others	Insecure Envious	That damn overbearing father who never thought I was good enough, damn his eyes, if I could get that old man back here from out of the grave for just one minute, I'd tell him …

The purpose of the Johari Window is to try to move the vertical line to the right so you have greater insight into yourself by finding out both your unconscious drivers and what other people think about you. If you are brave, you might want to lower the horizontal line too and open up to everyone. You can see how the idea of unknown unknowns springs directly from that bottom right quadrant.

The idea of unknown unknowns is also linked to unexpected or 'black swan' events. This phrase was coined by Nassim Taleb[102] to describe something no one predicts or plans for but which comes along anyway. It originated in European philosophy where a standard line in logic was 'all swans are white' because Europeans had only ever seen white swans … until they sailed to Western Australia and found many, many black swans.

The 2020 COVID-19 pandemic was often described as a 'black swan' event – an unknown unknown. But it wasn't. After SARS, MERS and Ebola in the previous two decades, governments, public health departments and those who followed current affairs knew, or should have known, that a pandemic was a possibility. There were pandemic response teams and organisations throughout the world. We might not have expected it, or liked what happened, but that's a whole other matter. COVID-19 was a known unknown. In the future, catastrophic climate change will not be a black swan event. Scientists have been warning about it for decades.

TRY IT OUT (IF YOU ARE GAME)

- Fill out half a Johari Window about yourself. Ask a partner or close friend to fill in the section 'known to others/not known to self'. Only do this if you are robust. What you read might be confronting.
- Try to fill out the known/unknown quadrant for the following issues (in each case you will have to leave the 'unknown unknown' category disturbingly blank):
  a. the impact of climate change
  b. the outcome of the next election in your country
  c. the internal and external factors that will affect your workplace's profitability in the next five years.

Avoiding the rush to judgement

You've opened that coffee shop on a main street and after two years it has failed. You sit alone at night, drinking sad shiraz out of your abandoned latte glasses, kicking yourself for not realising in advance all the things that went wrong. That barista who looked great on paper, was good at interview and came with sterling references, but turned out to be rude to the customers (you should have rung that fourth referee). The signature coffee bean from Kenya on which you staked your reputation got held up en route from Africa (you should have stuck with the local brand). The local council decided to rip up the pavement outside your shop and the jackhammers were deafening for three months (why didn't you check the council works schedule before you committed?). Then Starbucks opened down the road.

Before long you are convinced you are an idiot with rubbish judgement. You should never open a coffee shop again. The best you can hope for is a job cleaning the machines in more successful cafes owned by others.

But does this really stack up? Or have you made the judgement first ('the café failed because of my bad decisions') then cast around for supporting reasons in a form of self-hating confirmation bias? After all, could you have done much more to check out the barista you employed? How were you going to reliably assess the supply chain of the coffee bean? Sure, a really assiduous person might have checked out the local council's maintenance schedule, but most people would not have. And maybe Starbucks was just bad luck.

It is not great in any field of endeavour to start with your conclusion about a decision then search around for reasons that support it. This is rationalising, not reasoning. Generally, logic works the other way around – good reasons lead you *to* a conclusion. As the old saying goes, 'hindsight is 20/20'. Although many failures are an outcome of poor decisions or poor planning, others are the result of a hefty dose of bad luck or factors you couldn't see coming. (Conversely, some successes are not the result of business brilliance, but a hefty dose of good luck.)

This also matters in judging people in your organisation. Your IT specialist might have overseen the botched rollout of a software upgrade. However, keep the question open about whether they were to blame, or whether a multitude of factors meant it would have happened to anyone. Don't build a case – keep your mind open. You shouldn't suspend judgement but you shouldn't rush to judgement either.

This is a subset of how we handle risk. Much is made of visionaries who take risks and how this is a key part of their success. However, some risks just don't work out. You need to accept that, otherwise no one would ever take any risk. (This is not an excuse for the 'break things/fail fast' philosophy that wantonly hurts a lot of people on the way through.) It is also true for more mundane matters. When you go on a holiday to a beach resort you take the risk that the weather might be unseasonably lousy. If it rains for a week (providing it isn't monsoon season), don't make the judgement after the fact ('I never should have gone on this holiday, what an idiot'). You made a sound judgement in advance that came with inbuilt risk.

Linked to this is 'the historians' fallacy'. This is when people judge a past decision or policy harshly – but their main way of doing this is simply working backwards from a failed result. For example, the appeasement policy before World War II – when Britain did not stand up to Hitler's European land grabs in the 1930s – is today in the doggiest of doghouses in universities and high schools throughout the world. Yes, it failed – and what a spectacular, awful, unmitigated failure it was. But is it that unrelentingly unforgiveable in the context of the mid-1930s? Britain had been through a terrible war with Germany only 20 years earlier and seen a whole generation of its young men horribly killed in the trenches of World War I. Can politicians be truly blamed for deciding to go to great, even humiliating, lengths to avoid exterminating the next generation of young people? Hitler was already awful, but it was later that he became a 1-in-10,000-years level of awful. Or is the wisdom of hindsight – in this case the horrors of World War II and the Holocaust – skewing our judgement of the British Government's 1930s policy of appeasement?

Back to your failed coffee shop … yes, things fail, and they fail for reasons that become clear in hindsight. But don't make the mistake of loading onto a clear-eyed assessment of what went wrong the immediate scarifying judgement of 'I should have seen it coming'.

On the other hand, if your decision or project was a roaring success, it was obviously down to your singular brilliance and far-sightedness. Congratulations and well done.

TRY IT OUT

Reflect on how the rush to judgement has affected discussions or decisions in your life. If you can't think of any offhand, try:

- the post mortem undertaken by the losing party at the most recent election (they couldn't both win)
- the post mortem undertaken by the Blues or the Maroons in the most recent State of Origin Match (ditto)
- reflections on your child's most recent sporting season
- a decision that did not go well at work
- a recent holiday when something major went wrong
- the misdiagnosis of a health issue
- a movie that looked like it would be good but turned out to be a waste of time.

SIDEBAR: THE SIX THINKING HATS

When you are with a group of people trying to come up with a new product, set of ideas or way of doing things, thoughts can ricochet around the room: 'Why would we do this?'; 'People wouldn't buy this'; 'Yeah, but what's the evidence?'; 'This could be a game changer because …'; 'Could someone please take control of this meeting?' They are all valid cogitations, but they might tumble out in any order.

In 1985, thinking expert Edward de Bono devised a system to try to separate different types of thinking into different strands. He called them 'the six thinking hats'.[103]

The white hat denotes gathering information. De Bono picked this colour because it is like a blank sheet of paper that needs to be filled. It usually manifests as gathering facts. The questions you can ask using the white hat include 'What information do we already have?', 'What information is missing?' and 'How do we track down the information we need?' Piling up a bunch of facts to support your argument (rationalisation) is not a good use of information. Instead, the white hat encourages us to spread out the information we have to help make your argument or proposition (reasoning). Information can be facts, figures, lists, personal experience, scientific consensus, even deductions. Sometimes when tracking down information you have a laser-like focus. Other times you might go on a fishing expedition.

In those kinder, gentler days around 1985, information was more often unremarkable and thought to be neutral. Now it would pay to be careful about the information's truth, reliability and neutrality.

The red hat indicates feelings and hunches. De Bono chose this colour because red is usually associated with fire and warmth. It usually sounds like 'I don't know why, but I just have this real feeling that the time is right for this rollout'. What we call hunches can actually be a lifetime of experience and unconscious competence leading us to support a proposal or suggestion very quickly. We ignore feelings and emotional intelligence (EQ) at our peril. An important feature of red hat thinking is that people should not be asked to justify some of their thoughts, feelings or hunches, whether it's a part of a high-level meeting or a family discussion. They are feelings after all, and have their own validation.

Recent work by Daniel Kahneman has cast real doubt about using hunches instead of data, suggesting a hunch is just misguided confidence – but we have had a whole chapter about this in biases!

The yellow hat is the upside, possibility and positive future vision of any project. It is sunny optimism. De Bono got the colour from the sun. Broadly speaking, the questions associated with this hat are 'Why might it work?' and 'What are the benefits?' It is the 'benefits' segment of a 'cost/benefits' analysis. It is a way of looking at future projects.

Yellow hat thinking is not just wishful thinking. It is not much use thinking that climate change is going to be solved because it's a lovely day outside, or that ACME's perpetual motion machine is going to work because it would be fantastic to have something powering all our traffic. Yellow hat reasoning still needs to be logical and sound.

It is more rigorous than it first sounds. A project or idea must have clear and positively articulated benefits. If you cannot produce these, the idea cannot be very strong. There's little point in even getting into negative thinking if positive thinking does not provide a good case or benefit. In this event the idea is a non-starter.

The black hat is the 'downside' of any project. It's all the things that could go wrong, the pessimistic possibilities and the uncomfortable truths that bring the exciting 'big sky' thinking back to earth. De Bono picked black because it is like a black mark or the dress of a forbidding judge.

The black hat is the easiest to remember and by far the most well-known. Black hat thinking is an important check on exuberance and naïve optimism. The basic questions de Bono says you should ask using the black hat are 'Is it true?', 'Will it fit?' and 'Does it work?'

Black hat thinking is much more than just a whinge about change (although it can be that too). It can be the person who asks whether the facts presented are correct. It's the person who asks whether the evidence really allows you to make the conclusion you are making. It is a line of thinking that holds the group's analytical feet to the fire. Everyone should wear the proverbial black hat for a while – and everyone should take it off too.

The green hat is the creative or lateral thinking hat. It generates new, different or unexpected ways of tackling a problem. De Bono chose green to draw on the idea of new vegetation and new growth.

He categorises green hat thinking as explorations, proposals, suggestions, alternatives, new ideas and provocations. If you have a green hat thought, you don't have to come up with yellow and white hat reasons to support it. Instead, just put it out there to spin its wheels and give it a go.

Green hat ideas might possibly be considered outlandish or far-fetched. You might not want to seriously suggest them for fear you'll look like you don't have your feet on the ground. However, if you can raise these ideas under the cover of a green hat they can become more an accepted part of the process. And it is often green hat ideas and thinking that get people out of an ideas rut.

The blue hat is about how to organise the whole thinking discussion. If you are running the meeting, it's basically *how* you run the meeting. It is the bird's eye overview of the discussion where you can see and shape what is happening. De Bono got the idea from being up in the sky, looking down.

It is thinking about our thinking and decision making, so it this respect it is a 'meta-thinking' act. It is the sort of thinking that moderators and facilitators tend to stress. Blue hat thinking covers the questions 'Where are we now?', 'What is the next step?' and 'How can we sum up what we have been saying?'

The six hats can allow you to separate out the positive, the negative, fact finding and emotional thinking. They can also act as a checklist to make sure each type of thinking has been done in developing a new idea, process or product. Without all hats, it's easy to get an overly full head of steam or underemphasise data and facts.

The hats also help you get a team member out of a thinking rut and into other types of thinking. For example, everyone knows the person who is always happy to shoot ideas down. People can point out the value of black hat thinking but ask for some positives as well. The reverse is true of the idealistic yellow hat dreamer who never thinks about risk.

The six thinking hats became wildly popular several decades ago and the jargon of 'hats' became a part of many corporate cultures. It's likely you would only take this metaphor so far before it became overused. If Todd from marketing keeps saying, 'That's enough of your green hat thinking, Erica, why don't you try the white hat on for size', it might eventually become career limiting, as well as a personal safety issue for Todd. Regardless, as a mental check, an easy way of operating and a way of structuring a discussion, the concepts behind these hats still have a good deal of utility.

TRY IT OUT

Organise a brainstorming session in your head or with someone else using the six hats for these proposals:

- expanding your successful sushi restaurant into a chain of half-a-dozen stores
- using nuclear submarines as part of your country's defence force capabilities
- introducing a change to your workplace
- combining the 36 specialist IT platforms at your work, including several bespoke programs written by your own staff, into one all-purpose 'off-the-shelf' platform that appears to have the same functionality
- renovating your house or moving
- taking up the offer of Sam the virtual reality man to let you spend the rest of your life in a fantastic simulation that you will never know is not real.

CHAPTER 8

BEING A FAIR-MINDED THINKER

Thinking for yourself builds clarity and independence, which are both hugely significant in this era of ambiguity, strange reporting and disinformation. Thinking for yourself builds and amplifies confidence that you can construct well-founded beliefs and opinions and that you can respond to the beliefs and opinions of others. It will allow you to read, discuss, report, dispute, decide and vote with critical confidence. Thinking for yourself is about integrity, and integrity is built through review, reflection and rethinking. Seamus Heaney refers to this capacity to rest and return in thinking as 'the ground of convinced action, the basis of self-esteem and the guarantee of credibility in your lives, credibility to yourselves as well as to others'.[104]

If you are reading this handbook from start to end, you have read about peak end bias, which demonstrates that what is at the end of an experience tends to be what people remember the most. Because of that, we have left this section until last.

Throughout this book there are many ways to be a better thinker. But there is very little that would stop an unprincipled low-life from using these techniques and arguments to get their way over people who might be less sharp but more ethical. The use of these techniques to merely win an argument or convince people, instead of truly deliberating over an issue, is known as sophistry. Sophistry doesn't make society or the world any better. It often makes it worse. Similarly, using clear thinking to make effective decisions that unnecessarily harm others is immoral.

In using – not abusing – these critical thinking elements, your own intellectual character should come to the fore. This equates to your personal ethics. It is more difficult to write about these elements as they are more like ways of *being* than individual techniques. However, these elements of character will allow you to become a fair-minded thinker as well as a strong one. They can allow you to be vigilant about your own fair-mindedness and to expect it in others. The Foundation for Critical Thinking in the US is particularly focused on the centrality of intellectual character, and its founders Linda Elder and Richard Paul have done groundbreaking work in the field, building on a strong tradition that stretches back to John Dewey. We are reliant on their thinking on this topic.[105]

Valuable traits that relate to strong thinking include:

Humility: There are eight billion people on Earth. If we take an average, four billion of them could think at least as well as you do. Even if it is only one-tenth of that (putting you in the top five per cent of the population), there are still 400,000,000 people out there who think at least as well as you do – and some of them are probably in your neighbourhood, your workplace or in your family. Many will be writing the reputable newsfeeds, opinion articles, work reports and so on that we use to feed our own thinking. Some will sit opposite us in meetings. Many will be experts in their own areas in a way that we are not. Even if a person doesn't generally think as well as you do (particularly after you have read this book) they will still have invaluable and often better knowledge, experience or cultural awareness in particular areas.

All of this means it is better to walk into situations, arguments and discussions humbly. We should have a strong idea about what we can learn, how we can be better informed and what we can take away. The phrase 'I have one mouth and two ears' should often apply. We should be aware of our biases, and also that we probably have unconscious biases we aren't aware of yet – and might never be. We should be careful about the facts we really do know, and what we have merely taken for granted or assumed. Learning something back in high school doesn't mean it is rolled-gold accurate. Be willing to go back and check regularly.

Paradoxically, this will make our viewpoints and our conclusions stronger, not weaker. We will be more able to recognise our prejudices and collect facts we didn't know. We should be ready to be wrong at least some of the time (incidentally, always being right is a strong sign you are probably often wrong). We should be ready to continue to grow and learn as we change.

Courage: There are several types of courage. The first is the courage to delve into our own beliefs and be ready to fortify them, question them, adapt them or even change them if necessary. Really try to work out what makes the most sense rather than fall back on what you've believed or assumed previously. Linked to this is the courage to listen to opposing or different beliefs and a preparedness to take something from them. This is easier to do if we also have humility about our own beliefs.

We need the courage to sometimes question a belief shared by most of the people around us so we don't fall for 'groupthink'. Groupthink can happen in our family, our workplace, our community, our culture or our country. Courage does not mean iconoclastically going against the tide at every opportunity (this could just be vanity), but it does mean questioning what people around us might be taking for granted.

The second type of courage is being willing to defend and speak up for your belief once you think you have determined what is right. This can be difficult, because we are probably not 100 per cent convinced like the less reflective people on the other side of the table. But your view deserves a proper hearing. Of course, we need to take cues around us and consider the context. There is little point in loudly proclaiming your pro-choice, anti-gun views if you have just accidentally wandered into the main hall of the pro-life, pro-gun annual conference.

Most well-accepted ideas nowadays (democracy, same-sex rights) started life as unsupportable fringe concepts: all ideas have to start somewhere. However, beware of Galileo's gambit – most unsupportable fringe ideas also started as unsupportable fringe ideas. This is why the balance of courage and humility is so important.

We should not connect our personal identity too much with the individual beliefs we hold, such as our political leanings or our views about current issues. It would be better to connect our identity to the traits we value, such as courage and humility.

Empathy: Intellectual empathy involves literally or metaphorically sitting with another person and trying to understand why they think the way they do. It means putting ourselves in their place (as much as possible), with their experiences, their backgrounds and their views. Full empathy is difficult – we can't do a time-travel trick and quickly live the full span of their lives in order to completely understand their viewpoint. But we can use our own comparable experiences or sense of imagination to try to get some handle on it (and they should do the same for us).

Empathy helps you to reconstruct an event or an idea from another person's perspective and see what it looks like. When there are competing views in an argument or discussion about 'what happened' this can be invaluable. We should do it in good faith, not just to convince ourselves that the other person should have seen it our way all along.

The trick is to not let the uncertainty that comes from empathy and humility compromise fatally our ability to act. We will often have to make a call or judgement eventually regardless, even if the way forward is not as clear as we would like it. That's where the courage comes in.

Integrity: It is quite easy to hold other people to higher standards than we hold ourselves. Why aren't *they* changing their minds when presented with better evidence? Why are *they* jumping to conclusions? Why are *they* constructing and twisting the facts to fit with their opinion? Unfortunately, very few of us have the magical mental levitating power to lift ourselves above the flaws of everyone else. We're down there with them, although hopefully reading this book has given you a slight leg-up.

Intellectual integrity is about holding ourselves to at least the same standards to which we hold others. It's about examining our own flaws even as we accept other people's. It's also about putting ourselves through the same intellectual meat grinder we wish others would. It's about being kind and respectful to others' views (to a point), in the same way you would want them to be kind and respectful to yours. The focus on integrity is another take on the golden rule of 'do unto others as you would have done unto you'.

Integrity also is about your decisions and actions, acting in the way your beliefs dictate and not carving out exceptions for your own individual situation.

Resilience: Critical thinking can be hard. The ambiguity, the need for more information, the daily work of subjecting your beliefs and actions to scrutiny … it can make your head hurt. And that's before we get into those cognitive biases that show how 'naturally' we can fall into critical errors. It is very easy to simply fall back into comfortable, unexamined ways of thinking: 'I'm just fine, it will all work out'. You'll keep your friends, get along with your life and have a nice time down at the bar.

But really good thinking requires a perseverance that doesn't allow you to let your guard down very often. We need to be a friend to the frustration. Stuff isn't hard because it's worthless – stuff is often hard when it is worth *more*. The resilience needed to work through good thinking is important.

This can take time. A hard book read slowly is often worth more than two easy books read quickly. A sentence read twice is often worth twice as much as two sentences read once (read that again). Complexity does not come easily and that is what critical thinking is often about.

People are used to the idea of physical resilience – the idea of 'no pain, no gain' is deeply entrenched in exercise, sport and bodybuilding.

It is the same for our mind.

Reliance and autonomy: Sometimes we should rely heavily on other people for facts, opinions and judgements. If the judge of a long-running trial comes down in favour of or against a defendant, they are more likely to be right than us – after all, they have a law degree, they've had a career in law, and they've listened to the entire case. Climate change scientists have more expertise and considered opinions about the climate than most of us. Everywhere there are experts, experienced people, bosses, new recruits from other companies and other people with fresh new perspectives.

At the same time, there comes a moment when autonomy is required. When we have listened carefully, empathised deeply and respected the input of others, it is time to use our skills and ideas in our own unique way. This is, ultimately, the key to thinking for yourself. The arguments, views and perspectives you come up with will then be yours. You might end up with quite similar views and decisions to those around you, or they might be unique. What is important is that you made them yourself, soundly, independently and carefully.

AND SO, WE COME TO THE END ...

While we can't provide a rolled-gold guarantee that if you follow these thinking steps, your decisions will be superb, your opinions unimpeachable and your intellectual character the talk of the town, we do hope the many ideas you have already had about thinking over the decades have been collected, sharpened and made easier to use by this book. We hope you've learnt some completely new things about your thinking too.

This moment might just be a beginning. Adopting a deliberate strategy of thinking clearly should make you feel more confident about your decisions, shield you from the bad thinking of others and allow you to engage with public affairs more securely. That is no small combination. And there are plenty of great books about thinking. Some dive further into self-improvement; some are more elaborate explanations of fallacies or biases. We have digested many of them, and we hope you find those listed in the bibliography of use.

In getting to the end of this book, you have already done what most people won't. You have demonstrated that thinking is important to you and committed to giving it a mental workout to make it stronger. You have agreed not to be complacent and instead have said you will keep improving (that's not a future promise – that's a recognition of what you have already done by finishing this book). You are already a small but positive part of that great human enterprise that has continued collectively, century by century, millenium by millenium, away from ignorance, shortsightedness and prejudice into clarity, broad-mindedness and clear thinking. The path is still rocky, we might seem to take as many steps backwards as forwards, and whether we survive is going to be a close-run thing, but you are already on the side of the angels.

And if that is all a bit much, at least we hope it helps you choose the right car.

Good luck and go well.

Michael Parker and Fiona Morrison

APPENDIX: DEDUCTIVE REASONING

Formal logic and deductive reasoning are significant slices of the critical thinking pie. They take up about half of university textbooks about thinking and get very mathematical. This section might require a bit of slowing down, so here we go.

Deductive reasoning is the reverse of inductive reasoning: instead of starting with a statement and drawing a general conclusion (inductive), we start with general statements and try to draw a particular conclusion (deductive).

We can start with perhaps the most famous deductive piece of logic in history:

All people are mortal.
Socrates is a person.
Therefore, Socrates is mortal.

Neat, isn't it? The first two lines are called 'premises'. The third line is the 'conclusion'. Provided the first two lines are true in this form of the argument, then the third line will also be true. It's a rolled-gold guarantee.

You could strip this down further:

Premise 1: All P (people) are M (mortal)	All P are M
Premise 2: S (Socrates) is P (a person)	S is P
Conclusion: Therefore, S (Socrates) is M (mortal)	S is M

Once you have turned this reasoning into its base form, you can stick any other words into and it will still work. For example:

All people who read this book (P) want to know more about thinking (M)	All P are M
Sally (S) is a person who read this book (P)	S is P
Conclusion: Therefore, Sally (S) wanted to know more about thinking (M)	S is M

This deductive argument is called a 'syllogism'. It was first defined by Aristotle. Deductive reasoning is often about the 'form' of the argument being correct (or valid). It doesn't necessarily mean the argument is actually true (more on that soon).

Valid arguments and true premises

An argument is valid when the concluding statement *necessarily follows* from the premises. In a valid argument, if the premises are true, then the conclusion *has to* be true as well.

For example:

Premise 1: All people who eat beef (B) are carnivores (C)	All B are C
Premise 2: Donna (D) eats beef (B)	D is a B
Conclusion: Therefore, Donna is a carnivore.	D is a C

In this case there are both true premises and the 'proper form', and so the conclusion has to follow. Donna *has to be* a carnivore. This argument is also called 'sound' both because it is valid and because all the premises are true.

Valid arguments and false premises

In contrast, look at this argument, which is in exactly the same form and just as valid:

Premise 1: All people who eat beef (B) eventually turn into cows (C)	All B are C
Premise 2: Donna (D) eats beef (B)	D is a B
Conclusion: Therefore, Donna will eventually turn into a cow.	D is a C

The form is the same, which means the argument necessarily follows. It is still valid.[106]

It is also crazy.

Donna is not going to turn into a cow because she eats beef. She will remain human and not do even the slightest bit of ruminating. Yet the argument is still valid. The problem is that one of the premises is wrong. All people who eat beef do not eventually turn into cows. In fact, none of them do.

False premises can result in valid but untrue conclusions. For the conclusion to be sound – the holy grail of deductive reasoning – the form has to be valid and the premises have to be true.

Invalid arguments

Now let's try an invalid argument. These are even more difficult because they can have any number of true or false premises and true or false conclusions. Let's try the last example again with a slight twist:

Premise 1: All people who eat beef (B) are carnivores (C)	All B are C
Premise 2: Donna (D) is a carnivore (C)	D is a C
Conclusion: Therefore, Donna (D) eats beef (B)	D is a B

Do you see what we did there? This argument is very similar to the previous ones – there's just a tiny reverse of letters to change the premises. You almost don't notice it. But if you look carefully, it's there in the second premise – Donna is a 'C' (carnivore) instead of a 'B' (beef eater). The premises are still all true. But because of the letter swap the conclusion has changed. The conclusion now (that Donna eats beef) might or might not be true. Donna is still a carnivore. But she might or might not like beef. She might like the taste of pork but hate the taste of beef, or she may not be able to afford beef, so she only eats chicken. This becomes an invalid argument because the form changed, with a conclusion that may or may not be true.

TRY IT OUT

Which of the following arguments are valid? Which ones are sound?

A. Premise: All birds have feet.
   Premise: Canaries are birds.
   Conclusion: Therefore, canaries have feet.

B. Premise: All birds have feet.
   Premise: Dogs have feet.
   Conclusion: Therefore, dogs are birds.

C. Premise: All politicians are aliens from the planet Transfalmadore.
   Premise: Keir Starmer is a politician.
   Conclusion: Therefore, Keir Starmer is an alien from the planet Transfalmadore.

D. Premise: All boys have two heads.
   Premise: Jane has two heads.
   Conclusion: Therefore, Jane is a boy.

(Answer: A and C are valid. B and D are not. Only A is sound.)

ENDNOTES

Introduction

1 From 'English Language & Usage Stack Exchange': Quotes – '*A mind is like a parachute* – Who coined this expression, and when?', https://english.stackexchange.com/.
2 From 'World Economic Forum': *The Future of Jobs Report 2023*, https://www.weforum.org/publications/the-future-of-jobs-report-2023/.
3 Friedman, T. L., 'How to Get A Job at Google', *New York Times*, 2014.
4 Judge, M., 'Q&A: Garry Kasparov on the press and propaganda in Trump's America', *Columbia Journalism Review*, 2017.

Getting Started

5 From Halpern, D. F., *Thought and Knowledge: An introduction to critical thinking* (4th edn), Lawrence Erlbaum Associates, 2003, p. 2.
6 Dewey, J., *How we think*, D.C. Heath, 1910.
7 Glaser, E. M., *An Experiment in the Development of Critical Thinking*, New York: Teachers College, Columbia University, 1941.
8 From Norris, S. P., & Ennis, R. H. *Evaluating Critical Thinking*, Midwest Publications, 1989.
9 Facione, P. A., *Critical Thinking: A statement of expert consensus for purposes of educational assessment and instruction* (The Delphi Report), Millbrae, CA: California Academic Press, 1990.
10 Paul, R., & Elder, L., *Critical Thinking: Tools for taking charge of your learning and your life*, Upper Saddle River, NJ: Prentice Hall, (2001).
11 Halpern, D. F., op cit.
12 Rapp, C., 'Aristotle's Rhetoric', *The Stanford Encyclopedia of Philosophy* (Winter 2023 edn), Zalta, E. N., & Nodelman, U. (eds).
13 Smith, R, 'Aristotle's Logic', *The Stanford Encyclopedia of Philosophy* (Winter 2022 edn), Zalta, E. N. & Uri Nodelman (eds.).
14 Vickers, B., *In Defence of Rhetoric*, 1989, Oxford Scholarship Online 2011

15 Tan, C., 'A Confucian Conception of Critical Thinking' *Journal of Philosophy of Education*, Volume 51, Issue 1, February 2017, pp. 331–343.
16 Moore, B. and Parker, R., *Critical Thinking*, McGraw Hill Education, 2023, p 145.
17 Baggini J., *How to Think like a Philosopher*, Granta, 2023, p. 81.
18 From 'Voice of America News': 'Millions Still Believe the 1969 Moon Landing Was a Hoax', voanews.com.
19 Baggini J., op. cit.

Everyday Thinking about the World

20 From 'Oxford English Dictionary Online': Truth, n. & adv. meanings, etymology and more.
21 From 'Cambridge English Dictionary Online': fact.https://dictionary.cambridge.org/dictionary/english/fact.
22 Baggini J., op. cit., p. 28.
23 From Cambridge English Dictionary Online: https://dictionary.cambridge.org/dictionary/english/opinion
24 Lammel Heindel, C, 'Facts and Opinions' *Philosophy Now*, 2016 (August-September) https://philosophynow.org/issues/115/Facts_and_Opinion
25 Lammel Heindel, C, op.cit. https://philosophynow.org/issues/115/Facts_and_Opinion
26 From 'Cambridge English Dictionary Online': EVIDENCE | English meaning.
27 Arp, R., Barbone, S., and Bruce, M. (eds.), *Bad Arguments*, Wiley and Sons, 2018, p 3.
28 Fisher, A., op. cit., p.77.
29 Fisher, A., op. cit., p. 77.
30 Fisher, A., op. cit., p. 78.
31 Arp, R., Barbone, S., and Bruce, M. (eds.), op. cit., p. 138.
32 Moore B. and Parker R., op. cit., p. 114
33 Baggini J, op. cit., p. 231.
34 Cohen, M., *Critical Thinking Skills for Dummies*, Wiley, 2015, p. 179.
35 Cam P., *Twenty Thinking Tools: Collaborative Inquiry for the Classroom*, ACER Press, 2006.
36 From 'Factcheck.org': https://www.factcheck.org/2016/11/how-to-spot-fake-news/.
37 From 'Snopes': https://www.snopes.com/news/2016/01/21/6-quick-waysspot-fake-news/.
38 From 'The National Report': https://nationalreport.net/.
39 From 'Snopes': https://www.snopes.com/news/2016/01/21/6-quick-waysspot-fake-news/.
40 From Kruger, J., Dunning, D., 'Unskilled and Unaware of It: How Difficulties

in Recognizing One's Own Incompetence Lead to Inflated Self-Assessments', *Journal of Personality and Social Psychology*, January 2000, 77(6):1121-34.

41 Kruger, J., Dunning, D., op. cit., 1121-34.

42 De Bord, M., 'Americans are dangerously overconfident in their driving Skills – but they're about to get a harsh reality check', *Business Insider*, 2018: https://www.businessinsider.com.au/americans-are-overconfident-in-their-drivingskills-2018-1?r=US&IR==T

43 From Barry, C. M., 'Who Sharpened Occam's Razor?', *Irish Philosophy*, 27 May 2014.

44 Sagan, C., *Broca's Brain, Reflections on the Romance of Science*, Random House, 1979.

45 Dickinson, J. A., 'Lesser Spotted Zebras', *National Library of Medicine*, 2016.

46 Rawls, J., *A Theory of Justice*, Belknap Press, 1971.

47 Twain, M., 'Chapters from My Autobiography', *North American Review*, 1906.

48 Halpern, D., op.cit.

49 Halpern, D., op. cit., p 302.

50 From 'Our World in Data': The global decline of the fertility rate.

51 From: 'Statistics How To': https://www.statisticshowto.com.

52 From 'Statistics How To': https://www.statisticshowto.com/probability-andstatistics/descriptive-statistics/misleading-graphs/.

53 From 'Statistics How To': https://www.statisticshowto.com/wp-content/uploads/2014/01/usa-today-2.png.

Building More Skilful Arguments

54 Moore, B., and Parker R., op. cit., p. 41.

55 Arp, R., Barbone, S., and Bruce, M. (eds.), op. cit., p. 1.

56 Moore, B., and Parker R., op. cit., p. 6.

57 Arp, R., *Bad Arguments*, Wiley-Blackwell, 2018.

58 Moore, B., and Parker R., op. cit., p. 8.

59 Moore, B., and Parker R., op. cit., p. 10.

60 Moore, B., and Parker., R., op. cit. p. 10.

61 Moore, B., and Parker, R., op. cit., p. 10.

62 Arp, R, *Bad Arguments*, p. 2.

63 Halpern, D., op. cit., p. 189.

64 Halpern, D., op. cit., p. 189.

65 From 'Merriam-Webster': https://www.merriam-webster.com/dictionary/inference.

66 Halpern, D., op. cit., p.189.

67 Symes, A., and Robinson-McCarthy, L., *VCE Philosophy*, David Barlow Publishing, 2017, p. 22.

68 Halpern, D., op. cit., p. 195.

69 Halpern, D, op. cit., p. 199.

70 Kahneman, D., *Thinking, Fast and Slow*, Farrar, Straus and Giroux, 2011, p. 35.

Cognitive Biases

71 From University of Queensland: *How your brain makes and uses energy* – Queensland Brain Institute.

72 Kahneman, D., op. cit., p. 120.

73 Northcote Parkinson, C., *Parkinson's Law, or the Pursuit of Progress*, John Murray, 1958.

74 De Bord, M., 'Americans are dangerously overconfident in their driving Skills – but they're about to get a harsh reality check', Business Insider, 2018, https://www.businessinsider.com.au/americans-are-overconfident-in-their-drivingskills-2018-1?r=US&IR=T.

Thinking Fallacies of Relevance

75 From Goodwin, J., 'Forms of Authority and the Real Ad Verecundiam', Argumentation, 1998, 12(2) 267-280.

76 Oreskes, N. 'Beyond the Ivory Tower: The Scientific Consensus on Climate Change',Science, 2004, 306, 1686.f.

77 Sagan, C., *The Demon-Haunted World, Science as a Candle in the Dark*, Random House Group, 1997, p. 31.

78 Clinton in interview with Dan Rather, CBS News, 13 September 2001, quoted in Cunningham, E.M., 'Understanding Rhetoric: A Guide to Critical Reading and Argumentation'.

79 Bush, G. W., *Address to a joint session of Congress and the American people*, The White House, 20 September 2001, https://georgewbush-whitehouse.archives.gov/news/releases/2001/09/20010920-8.html.

80 Arp R., Barbone, S., and Bruce, M. (eds.), op. cit.

81 From 'American Rhetoric': https://www.americanrhetoric.com/speeches/richardnixoncheckers.html.

82 Mill, J. A., *A System of Logic, Ratiocinative and Inductive*, Cambridge University Press, 1843 (2011 edn).

83 From 'Psychology Today': https://www.psychologytoday.com/au/blog/logicaltake/202006/the-galileo-gambit-and-appealing-ignorance.

84 Arp R., Barbone, S., and Bruce, M. (eds.), op. cit., p.155.

85 Sagan, C., *Broca's Brain*, op. cit., p. 64.

86 Klement, K., 'When Is Genetic Reasoning Not Fallacious?', University of Massachusetts.

87 Schwartzstein, P., 'The History of Poisoning The Well', *Smithsonian Magazine*, 2019.

88 Arp, R., Barbone, S., and Bruce, M. (eds.), op. cit., p. 197.

89 Arp., R., Barbone, S., and Bruce, M. (eds.), op. cit., p. 199.

Thinking Fallacies of Presumption

90 Warburton, N., *Thinking from A to Z* (3rd edn), p 132, Routledge, 2007.
91 Moore, B., and Parker, R., op. cit., p. 404.
92 Flew, A., *God & Philosophy*, Hutchinson,1966, p. 104.
93 Wendell Homes Jr, O., in *Schenck v. United States*, 1919.
94 Arp, R., Barbone, S., and Bruce, M. (eds.), op. cit., p. 349.

Making Good Decisions

95 Parrish, S., *Clear Thinking*, Penguin, 2023.
96 Fisher, A., *Critical Thinking, An Introduction* (2nd edn), Cambridge University Press, 2011, p. 17.
97 Fitzgerald, F. S., 'The Crack Up', *Esquire Magazine*, February 1936, p. 41.
98 Smith, W., Lewis, M., Tushman, M., '"Both/And" Leadership', Harvard Business Review, May 2016.
99 Covey, S. R., *The 7 Habits of Highly Effective People: Restoring the Character Ethic* (rev. edn.), Simon and Schuster, 2004.
100 Rumsfeld, D., *Known and Unknown*, Penguin, 2010, p. 13.
101 Luft, J., *Of Human Interaction*, National Press Books, 1969, p. 177.
102 Taleb, N., 'The Black Swan: The Impact of the Highly Improbable' (2nd edn), Penguin, 2011.
103 De Bono, E., *Teach Your Child How to Think*, Viking, 1992.

Being a Fair-Minded Thinker

104 Bark, S. (ed), *Take this Advice: The best graduation speeches ever given*, Gallery Books, 2006.
105 Paul, R., and Elder, L., *Critical Thinking* (2nd Edition), 2014.

Appendix: Deductive Reasoning

106 Symes, A., and Robinson-McCarthy, L., *VCE Philosophy*, David Barlow Publishing, 2017, p. 39.

FURTHER READING

Ahn, W., *Thinking 101: Lessons in Clarity, Focus and Making Better Decisions*, Macmillan Business, 2022

Arp, R., Barbone, S. & Bruce, M., *Bad Arguments: 100 of the Most Important Fallacies in Western Philosophy*, Wiley Blackwell, 2019

Baggini, J., *How to Think Like a Philosopher*, Granta, 2023

Bailey, S. and Black, O., *Mind Gym*, Harper, 2014

Brockman, J. (ed), *Thinking*, HarperCollins, 2013

Cam, P., *Philosophical Inquiry: Combining the Tools of Philosophy With Inquiry-Based Teaching and Learning*, Rowman and Littlefield, 2020

Cam, P., *Twenty Thinking Tools*, ACER Press, 2006

Cohen, M., *Critical Thinking for Dummies*, Wiley and Sons, 2015

De Bono, E., *Teach Your Child How to Think*, Viking, 1992

Dennet, D., *Intuition Pumps and Other Tools for Thinking*, Penguin, 2014

Dewey, J., *How We Think*, Dover Publications, 1998 (first published 1910)

Dobelli, R., *The Art of Thinking Clearly*, Sceptre, 2013

Elder, L. & Paul, R., *The Thinker's Guide to Analytic Thinking*, Foundation for Critical Thinking Press, 2016

Ennis, R. H., *Critical Thinking*, Pearson Education, 1996

Facione, P., '*Critical Thinking: What It Is and Why It Counts*', California Academic Press, 2010

Fisher, A., *Critical Thinking: An Introduction*, Cambridge University Press, 2011

Foresman, G., Fosl, P. & Watson, J., *The Critical Thinking Toolkit*, Wiley-Blackwell, 2017

Halpern, D., *Critical Thinking Across the Curriculum*, Routledge, 1997

Halpern, D., *Thought and Knowledge*, Lawrence Erlbaum Associates, 2003

Harvard Business School Publishing Corporation, *HBR Guide to Critical Thinking*, Harvard Business Review Press, 2023

Kallet, M., *Think Smarter: Critical Thinking to Improve Problem-Solving and Decision-Making Skills*, Wiley and Sons, 2014

Kahneman, D., *Thinking, Fast and Slow*, Farrar, Straus and Giroux, 2011

Martin, R., *There Are Two Errors in the the Title of This Book**, Broadview Press, 2002

McMillan, K. & Weyers, J., *How to Improve Your Critical Thinking and Reflective Skills*, Pearson Education, 2013

Moore, B. & Parker, R., *Critical Thinking*, McGraw Hill Education, 2021

Nadler, S. & Shapiro, L., *When Bad Thinking Happens to Good People*, Princeton University Press, 2021

Nosich, G., *Critical Writing*, Rowman and Littlefield, 2022

Parrish, S., *Clear Thinking: The Art and Science of Making Better Decisions*, Penguin, 2023

Paul, R. & Elder, L., *Critical Thinking: Tools for Taking Charge of Your Learning and Your Life,* Pearson Education, 2014

Paul, R. & Elder, L., *Critical Thinking: Learn the Tools the Best Thinkers Use*, Rowman and Littlefield, 2006

Pirie, M., *How to Win Every Argument*, Bloomsbury Academic, 2015

Rawls, J., *A Theory of Justice*, Bellknap Press, 1971

Sagan, C., *Broca's Brain: Reflections on the Romance of Science*, Random House, 1979

Sagan, C., *The Demon-Haunted World: Science as a Candle in the Dark*, Hodder Headline, 1996

Symes, A. & Robinson-McCarthy, L., *VCE Philosophy*, David Barlow Publishing, 2013

Taleb, N., *The Black Swan: The Impact of the Highly Improbable (Second Edition)*, Penguin, 2011

Warburton, N., *Thinking from A to Z*, Routledge, 2007

ACKNOWLEDGEMENTS

Many people have helped us on a critical thinking journey that has spanned several decades now. We appreciate and thank them all.

Philip Cam and Sandra Lynch have done so much over the decades in Australia to promulgate and promote philosophy and thinking with young people. Their own writings and teachings have been instrumental. Our dozens (or was it hundreds?) of meetings over three decades with the Philosophy in Schools Association laid so much groundwork.

In times gone by, Bruce Carter, Michael Smee and Jeff Snare made educational time and space available to write and promote this material. More recently, thank you to Tony McDonald and the Council of Newington College for sabbatical time that helped bring this book finally together. The Critical Thinking Centre and Ethics Centre at Newington has some excellent colleagues and facilitators. Particular thanks go to Britta Jensen as the Director of the Centre, and also to Kate Kennedy White, Jeremy Hall, Mark Case, Amy Van Arkkels, Victoria Howe, Andrew Constantino, Sam Giles and Janine Timillero. Thank you, too, to Professor Michael Balfour, Head of the School of the Arts and Media at UNSW Sydney for his support over the years.

Some of the most expert critical thinking people in the world have been generous with their time and perspectives – sometimes spending whole days with strangers who turn up at their door asking about critical thinking. We thank the generosity of Brooke Moore, Linda Elder, AC Grayling, Diane Halpern, Edward de Bono (deceased) and Peter Ellerton.

Thank you to our wonderful publisher Jane Curry for her unstinting confidence in us and for making this all happen. To Annie Markey for her expert comments and editing. To Amanda Hemmings, Managing Editor, and all who helped with the production process.

Closer to home, thank you to Julia Parker and Elena Parker for their comments and unwavering support. To Indigo – all four kilos of Cavoodle that she is. To our families and friends for keeping us connected and for ensuring we don't start spouting critical thinking vignettes in the middle of dinner at a Thai restaurant. We appreciate it.

All author royalties from this book will go to the Chris Wild Indigenous Scholarship fund at Newington College.

INDEX

20 Thinking Tools (book), 22
60-40 decisions, 4, 6, 228–30
9/11 attacks, 151

A
abductive reasoning, 25, 28–30
four criteria for, 28–29
AC/DC method, 37–38
ad hominem argument *see* fallacies of relevance – attacking the person
advocatus diaboli *see* devil's advocate
affirming the consequent (fallacy), 34, 35
AI *see* artificial intelligence
AI-generated images, 9, 73
analogy *see* false analogies,
analytical definitions, 98
anchoring effect, 4, 117–19, 143
anviksiki, 21
appeasement, 242–43
argument from design *see* William Paley
argument from false authority (fallacy), 5, 147–49
argument from purity *see* fallacies of presumption – no true Scotsman
arguments, 20, 50, 60, 81
  assessing *see* Halpern method,
  building, 93–105
  claims, 95
  conclusions, 95–97
  definition of, 93
  definitions in, 97–98
issues, 99
premises, 95–97
sound, 259, 260
valid, 36, 101, 258–60
see also AC/DC method; counterargument; evidence; reasoning, types of
arguments from emotion *see* fallacies of relevance
Aristotle, 3, 20, 21, 42, 78, 189, 258
Arp, Robert, 54, 99
Asch, Solomon, 136
assumptions, 6, 37, 102–03, 146
  hidden, 102, 145, 195
  see also fallacies of presumption
autonomy, trait in reasoning, 10, 254
availability bias, 5, 115–16, 143
availability cascade *see* availability bias
availability effect *see* cognitive biases – availability cascade
averages *see* statistics median, mean

B
Baggini, Julian, 28, 37–38, 46,
balance of probabilities, 58, 59, 60
base rate fallacy, 113
begging the question (fallacy), 189–91
Bible, the, 21, 23
Big Bang, the, 57, 184
'bike shed effect' (cognitive bias), 130–31
'black swan' events, 6, 239–406
Bock, Laszlo, 7
both/and thinking, 151, 218, 219–21
bots, 9
burden of proof, 58, 61
Bush, George, 151

C
California, 22
Cam, Philip, 22, 68, 269
cancel culture, 201
celebrity endorsement *see* fallacies of relevance – argument from false authority; cognitive biases – halo effect
Centre for Critical Thinking, 22
ChatGPT, 12
circular reasoning *see* fallacies of presumption – begging the question
circumstantial evidence *see* direct vs circumstantial evidence
claims, *see* arguments
Clarke, Arthur C., 29
clichés *see* fallacies of presumption – clichés
climate change debate, 53, 83, 124, 148, 165, 240, 245, 254
Clinton, Hillary, 151
cognitive biases, 109–43, 245, 251, 253, 255
  'bike shed effect', 130–31
  anchoring effect, 4, 117–19, 143
  availability cascade, 115–16, 143
  base rate fallacy, 113
  confirmation bias, 109, 135–39
  framing bias, 128–29
  halo effect, 135, 136–37
  illusion of validity, 134
  law of small numbers, 5, 124–25
  less is more *see* base rate fallacy
  peak end bias, 140–42, 143
  planning fallacy, 110, 120–21
  priming effect, 122–23
  regret bias, 132–33, 143
  resemblance bias, 113–14
  sunk cost fallacy, 109, 126–27
  what you see is all there is, 138–39
coherence *see* abductive reasoning – four criteria; coherence theory of truth
coherence theory of truth, 43
comprehensiveness *see* abductive reasoning – four criteria
conditional (if/then) reasoning, 32–35
  affirming the consequent, 34
  denying the antecedent, 33
  modus ponens, 32–33
  modus tollens, 33–34
confirmation bias, 109, 135–39
Confucianism, 21
Connery, Sean, 68–69
consistency, 4, 104–05, 216–20, 223
'consistent inconsistency', 220
logical, 217
practical, 217
'consistent inconsistency', 220
conspiracy theories, 29–30, 47, 59, 72, 184
  moon landing, 29–30
  flat earthism, 1–2, 27, 47, 164, 184
  UFOs, 184
  climate denialism, 47
  See also hoaxes
contestability, 50
contingent beliefs, 50

core skills for workers, 8
correlation, vs causation, 185; *see also* post hoc ergo propter hoc
correspondence theory of truth, 43
counterarguments, 4, 100, 159, 183
counterexamples, 68, 192
courage, trait in reasoning, 10, 251–52, 253
Covey, Stephen, 233
COVID-19 pandemic, 240
credibility, 6, 19, 62–64, 249
criteria, 4, 5, 210–12, 214, 228
  for abductive reasoning, 28–29
  for decision-making, 210–12
  vs rules, 211
critical thinking
  application of, 4–6,
  benefits, 7–12
  challenges to, 2, 12–13, 40–41; *see also* cognitive biases
  definitions of, 17–19
  history of, 20–23
  terminology, 23–24
  difficulty of formalising, 37
  valuable traits for, 250–54
critique, 24
cum hoc ergo propter hoc (fallacy), 186–87
Curie, Marie, 3

D

Darwin, Charles, 23, 75, 76
de Bono, Edward, 244–48, 270
decision making, 9–10, 17, 19, 26, 41, 47, 51, 58, 59, 67, 109, 112, 126–27, 130, 131, 133, 139, 143, 146, 153, 205–43, 247, 255
  criteria for, 210–12
  prioritisation, 232–35
  steps for, 206
deductive reasoning, 25, 26, 36, 55, 257–60
deep fakes, 9
definition by example, 98
definition by synonym, 98
definitions
  types of, 98
  good definitions, 98
democracy, 8–9, 45, 83, 252
denominator, 85–86
denying the antecedent (fallacy), 33, 34, 35
Descartes, René, 45–46
devil's advocate, 4, 81–83
Dewey, John, 17, 18, 250
circumstantial evidence, 55–56
disinformation, 2, 9, 71, 249
distinctions
drawing distinctions, 4, 38, 222–25
false distinctions, 224
domino effect *see* fallacies of presumption – slippery slope
Dunning, David, 75
Dunning-Kruger effect, 75–76

E

echo chamber effect, 41, 72, 81, 83
Einstein, Albert, 3, 147, 200
Eisenhower, Dwight D., 159, 233
either/or thinking *see* both/and thinking),
Elder, Linda, 10, 19, 22, 250, 270
emotional intelligence (EQ), 245
empathy, trait in reasoning, 10, 252–53
Ennis, Robert, 18
epistemology, 46, 174; *see also* truth, theories of
euphemisms, 197
evidence, 1, 5, 17, 25, 26, 28, 30, 38, 43, 48, 54–64, 99–100, 135, 165, 253
  circumstantial, 55–56
  definition of, 54
  direct sensory, 54

direct, 55
evaluating, 52, 62–64
expert testimony, 55, 62–64
indirect sensory, 54
logical/mathematical proofs,
original vs hearsay, 56
rationalisation, 81
scientific explanation, 55, 165
standard of, 58–60, 79, 99–100, 211
trusted testimony, 54-55
see also facts; opinion of evaluation; premises
excluded middle (fallacy), 150–02
'experience machine', 45–46
experts
argument from authority, 148
credibility of, 62–64, 148–49
testimony, 55, 62–64
explanation, 20, 28–29, 103
authoritative, 55
simplicity *see* Occam's razor
see also abductive reasoning
extrapolation (fallacy) *see* fallacies of relevance – extrapolation
extrapolation (in statistics), 89

F

Facione, Peter, 19,
FactCheck.org, 71, 73
facts, 1, 5, 29, 37, 38, 45–49, 50, 51–52, 62, 71, 73, 85, 128, 139, 147, 219, 222, 244, 246, 251
and opinion, 51–52
and truth, 42–43
definition of, 45
nature of, 45–49
see also false facts
fake news, 43, 70–74
fallacies of presumption, 145, 179– 201
begging the question, 189–91
clichés, argument-ending, 200–01
cum hoc ergo propter hoc, 186–87
free speech argument, 200–01
loaded question, 195–96
'no true Scotsman', 192–94
post hoc ergo propter hoc, 186–88
shifting the goalposts *see* 'no true Scotsman'
slippery slope, 4, 179–82
unfalsifiability, 183–85, 192
weasel words, 197–99
fallacies of relevance, 145–77
argument from emotion, 153–54
attacking the person, 155–57, 168, 174
excluded middle, 150–52
false analogy, 161–63
false authority, 5, 147–49
Galileo gambit, 5, 164–66, 252
genetic fallacy, 170–72, 173
hollow man argument, 159
poisoning the well, 5, 173–75
red herring, 167–69
special pleading, 176–77
straw man argument, 158–60
unfair extension, 159–60
weak man argument, 159
fallacy, 33–34, 145–201
definition, 145
types of, 145
historians' fallacy, 242–42
denying the antecedent, 33, 34
affirming the consequent, 34
see also cognitive bias
fallacy of origin *see* genetic fallacy
false analogy (fallacy), 161–63
false authority (fallacy), 5, 147–49
false facts, 43, 71; *see also* fake news
falsifiability,
Fisher, Alec, 207
Fitzgerald, F. Scott, 219–20
flat-earthism, 1–2, 27, 47, 164, 184
Flew, Antony, 192
floodgates effect *see* fallacies of

presumption – slippery slope
formal logic *see* deductive reasoning
Foundation for Critical Thinking, 250
framing bias, 128–29
free speech *see* fallacies of presumption – free speech argument
Future of Jobs Report 2023, 7, 8

G
Galileo gambit (fallacy), 5, 164–66, 252
Gantt chart, 234–35
Gantt, Henry, 234
generalisation, 67–70, 192
  countering, 68–79
  prejudice and, 67–68
  qualifying, 69
genetic fallacy, 170–72, 173
Glaser, Edward, 18
Google, 7, 11
Gorgias (Plato), 21
grammar, 75; *see also* passive voice
graphs, 89–91
Greek philosophy, 20; *see also* Aristotle; Socrates; Plato
Gulf War, 183–84

H
halo effect (cognitive bias), 135, 136–37
Halpern method, the, 104–06
Halpern, Diane, 19, 22, 85, 89, 101, 104
Harvard University, 128–29
Heaney, Seamus, 249
hearsay, 56
hidden assumptions, 102, 145, 195
hindsight, 241, 243
historians' fallacy, 242–43
hoaxes, 47,
  New York Sun, 71
  see also conspiracy theories; disinformation; fake news; false facts; misinformation;
Holiday, Ryan, 187
hollow man argument (fallacy), 159
Human Rights Foundation, 9
humility, trait in reasoning, 10, 146, 250–51, 252, 253

I
illusion of validity (cognitive bias), 134
Indian philosophy, 21
inductive reasoning, 25–27, 67, 257
  cogency in, 26–27
inductive truths, 42, 45
inference, 19, 28, 101–02, 146
information, 39–44
  assessing sources, 62–64
  democratisation of, 40
  evaluating credibility, 62–64
  history of dissemination, 39–41
  weaponisation of, 41
  see also evidence; facts; unknown unknowns
Ingham, Harrington, 238
integrity, intellectual, trait in reasoning, 10, 146, 249, 253
internet, 9, 40, 54, 72, 73
Irving, Kyrie, 187
ISIS, 155, 173

J
Johari Window, 238–39
Johnson, David Kyle, 165

K
Kahneman, Daniel, 22–23, 109–10, 111, 113, 118, 120–21, 125, 134, 140, 143, 245
Kasparov, Garry, 9
Klement, Kevin, 171
Kruger, Justin, 75
Kubrick, Stanley, 29

L
Lammer-Heindel, Christoffe, 52
law of small numbers, 5, 124–25
law of triviality *see* cognitive biases – 'bike shed effect'
legal reasoning, 55–56
Lindy Chamberlain case, 51–52
Lipman, Matthew, 22
literary criticism, 24
loaded question (fallacy), 195–96
Locke, John, 147
logic, 9, 18, 20–22, 25, 36, 42, 55, 110, 239, 241; *see also* deductive reasoning; inductive reasoning
logical consistency, 217
logos (Greek), 20
Luft, Joseph, 238

M
mainstream media, 40, 71, 72, 73
mathematics, 7, 21, 22, 25, 55, 89, 93, 257
mean, 86–88
  regression to, 37, 87–88, 143
  vs median, 86
median, 86–87
Middle Ages, 21
Mill, John Stuart, 161
misinformation, 71–74, 149
  resources for checking, 71–72
  vs disinformation, 71, 73
modus ponens, 32–33
modus tollens, 33–34
Moore, Brooke, 22, 94, 96, 98, 270
motivation, 63
Moynihan, Daniel, 48

N
necessary and sufficient conditions, 213–15
Nixon, Richard, 158–59
'no true Scotsman' (fallacy), 192–94
Nobel Prize, 22
Nosich, Gerald, 19

O
objectivity, 42, 43–44, 51, 205
Occam's razor, 78–80
Octavian (Augustus), 71
opinions, 1, 4, 6, 9, 12, 43, 44, 47–48, 50–53, 71, 77, 81–83, 94, 95, 99, 217, 249, 254
  expert, 148, 254
  of evaluation, 51
  of fact, 51–52
  of preference, 51
  see also subjectivity
Oreskes, Naomi, 148
Organon (Aristotle), 20

P
Paley, William, 162
paradox, 219–20
Parker, Richard, 22, 94, 96, 98
Parkinson, Cyril Northcote, 130
Parrish, Shane, 206
passive voice, 198
Pasteur, Louis, 165
Paul, Richard, 10, 19, 22, 250
peak end bias, 140–42, 143
Pericles, 9
petitio principii *see* fallacies of presumption – begging the question
Petraeus, David, 155
Phaedrus (Plato), 21
Philosophy in Schools movement, 22
physiological basis of thought, 22
planning fallacy (cognitive bias), 110, 120–21
Plato, 20–21
plausibility *see* standard of proof – reasonably plausible
poisoning the well (fallacy), 5, 173–75
PolitiFact.com, 73

post hoc ergo propter hoc (fallacy), 186–88
practical consistency, 217
pragmatic theory of truth, 43
precedent *see* consistency
prejudice, 67–68, 226, 251, 255
priming effect (cognitive bias), 122–23
print media, 40,
prioritisation, 4, 228, 232–35
urgency vs importance, 232–34
matrices, 233
see also Gantt chart
probable cause *see* standard of proof

Q
quadrivium, 21
qualifiers, 69, 101

R
ratio (Latin), 21
rationalisation, 81
Rawls, John, 82
reasoning, types of
abductive, 25, 28–30
conditional, 32–35
deductive, 25, 26, 36, 55, 257–60
inductive, 25–27, 67, 257
red herring (fallacy), 167–69
Redelmeier, Don, 140
reflective thinking, 17, 18
regret bias, 132–33, 143
reliance, trait in reasoning, 254–55
religion, 20, 147, 171, 192
Renaissance, 21
resemblance bias, 113–14
resilience, trait in reasoning, 10, 253–54
Rhetoric (Aristotle), 20
rhetoric, 20–21
  Rogerian, 21–22
risk, 132, 208–09, 237–38, 242
Rogerian rhetoric, 21–22
Ruiz, Roberto, 174
Rumsfeld, Donald, 236
Russell, Bertrand, 15

S
Sagan, Carl, 79, 148, 165–66
Salem witch trials, 174
sample size, 86
Schwarz, Norbert, 116
science, 22, 23–24, 47, 55, 78, 148–49, 164–65, 184, 244
climate, 83, 148, 254
speculative, 184
sensory evidence, 54
Sharp, Ann Margaret, 22
shifting the goalposts (fallacy) *see* 'no true Scotsman'
simplicity *see* abductive reasoning – four criteria; Occam's Razor
six thinking hats, 244–48
slippery slope (fallacy), 4, 179–82
Smith, Wendy, 220
Snopes.com, 71, 72, 73
social media, 2, 40–41, 71, 74, 94, 62, 162, 200
  horizontality of, 62
Socrates, 20, 21
special pleading (fallacy), 176–77
Sports Illustrated jinx, 87
standard of proof
  balance of probabilities, 58–59, 165
  beyond reasonable doubt, 59, 165
  clear and convincing evidence, 59–60
  reasonable plausibility, 60
statistics, 26–27, 69, 84–92, 99, 110
  denominator, 85–86
  extrapolation, 89
  fake precision, 88–89
  in graphs, 89–91
  mean, 86–88
  median, 86–87

regression to the mean, 37, 87–88, 143
sample size, 86
see also base rate fallacy; law of small numbers
stereotypes, 68
Stoicism, 187
straw man argument (fallacy), 158–60
subjectivity, 43–44; *see also* opinions
sunk cost fallacy (cognitive bias), 109, 126–27
syllogism, 258
system 1 and 2 thinking, 110–13, 138

T
Taleb, Nassim, 239
testability *see* abductive reasoning – four criteria; unfalsifiability
Thaler, Richard, 132
Washington Post Fact Checker, 73
thin end of the wedge *see* fallacies of presumption – slippery slope
Thinking, Fast and Slow (book), 23, 110, 113
thought experiments, 68; *see also* hypotheticals
trivium, 21
troll farms, 9
trust, 54–55, 62, 64, 74, 148
truth, theories of
correspondence theory, 43
coherence theory, 43
pragmatic theory, 43
tu quoque argument *see* fallacies of relevance – attacking the person
Turnbull, Malcolm, 155
Tversky, Amos, 22, 109
Twain, Mark, 89
Tyson, Neil deGrasse, 189

U
UNESCO, 71
unfair extension (fallacy), 159–60
unfalsifiability, 182–85, 192
unknown unknowns, 236–39

V
validity
formal, 36, 101, 258–60
illusion of *see* cognitive biases – illusion of validity
veil of ignorance *see* John Rawls

W
Wag the Dog (film), 168
Wainer, Howard, 125
Warburton, Nigel, 181
weak man argument (fallacy), 159
weasel words (fallacy), 197–99
Wegener, Alfred, 165
what you see is all there is (WYSIATI) (cognitive bias), 138–39
William of Ockham, 78
World Economic Forum, 7
Wrisley, George, 155

Z
Zappa, Frank, 1
Zwerling, Harris, 125